THE ECLIPSE OF THE SUN

THE ECLIPSE OF THE SUN

The Need for American Indian Curriculum in High Schools

ROBERTA CAROL HARVEY

SUNSTONE PRESS
SANTA FE

© 2022 by Roberta Carol Harvey
All Rights Reserved
No part of this book may be reproduced in any form or by any electronic or mechanical means including information storage and retrieval systems without permission in writing from the publisher, except by a reviewer who may quote brief passages in a review.

Sunstone books may be purchased for educational, business, or sales promotional use. For information please write: Special Markets Department, Sunstone Press, P.O. Box 2321, Santa Fe, New Mexico 87504-2321.

Book and cover design › R. Ahl
Printed on acid-free paper
∞
eBook 978-1-61139-685-0

Library of Congress Cataloging-in-Publication Data

Names: Harvey, Roberta Carol, 1950- author.
Title: The eclipse of the sun : the need for American Indian curriculum in high schools / Roberta Carol Harvey.
Description: Santa Fe : Sunstone Press, [2022] | Includes bibliographical references and index.
Identifiers: LCCN 2022027852 | ISBN 9781632933959 (paperback) | ISBN 9781611396850 (epub)
Subjects: LCSH: Indians of North America--Education--Law and legislation--Colorado. | Education--Curricula--Colorado. | Indians of North America--Colorado--Government relations. | Indians of North America--Colorado--Social conditions. | Multicultural education--Colorado.
Classification: LCC E97.65.C6 H37 2022 | DDC 371.829/970788--dc23/eng/20220719
LC record available at https://lccn.loc.gov/2022027852

WWW.SUNSTONEPRESS.COM
SUNSTONE PRESS / POST OFFICE BOX 2321 / SANTA FE, NM 87504-2321 /USA
(505) 988-4418 / FAX (505) 988-1025

Dedication

To the Indian Parent who stood up for minority students' rights, as a matter of simple justice. A law existed that needed to be complied with for their well-being. The U.S. Civil Rights Commission noted in 2018 that the "lack of appropriate cultural awareness in school curriculum focusing on Native American history or culture" can (1) be harmful to American Indian students; (2) contribute to a negative learning environment; (3) be isolating and limiting; (4) trigger bullying; and (5) result in negative stereotypes across the board.

The same is true for all minority students.

Institutional Racism

Institutional racism has a life of its own. It does not need to be perpetuated. It is, by definition as being institutionalized, self-perpetuating. It no longer needs to find a host to propagate; it is airborne.

"Institutional racism is often the most difficult to recognize and counter, particularly when it is perpetrated by institutions and governments who do not view themselves as racist. When present in a range of social contexts, this form of racism reinforces the disadvantage already experienced by some members of the community. For example, racism experienced by students at school may result in early school dropout and lower educational outcomes. Together with discrimination in employment, this may lead to fewer employment opportunities and higher levels of unemployment for these students when they leave school. In turn, lower income levels combined with discrimination in the provision of goods and services restrict access to housing, health care and life opportunities generally. In this way, institutional racism may be particularly damaging for minority groups and further restrict their access to services and participation in society." See www:racismnoway.com.au/classroom/Factsheet/32.html.

CONTENTS

21 / Acknowledgments

23 / PART 1 / Introduction

26 / PART 2 / Community Concerns with Non-Inclusive Curriculum, Including American Indians

    26 / Indigenous Community Concerned with CCSD's Non-Inclusive Curriculum
    27 / CCSD's Students' Concerned with CCSD's Non-Inclusive Curriculum
    30 / Denver's Public School's Black Students Concerned with Non-Inclusive Curriculum
    31 / Other Minorities Concerned with CCSD's Non-Inclusive Curriculum
    31 / African-American Community Concerned with CCSD's Non-Inclusive Curriculum
    31 / Asian-American Community Concerned with CCSD's Non-Inclusive Curriculum
    33 / Latin Community Concerned with Need for More Inclusive Curriculum Statewide
    33 / LGBTQ Community Concerned with Need for More Inclusive Curriculum Statewide
    34 / Site after Site on the Internet Proclaim Colorado Law Mandating LGBTQ Inclusion in Curriculum
    34 / White Community Divided Over Need for More Inclusive Curriculum, CCSD BOE Meeting, June 23, 2021
    35 / Need for Civics Education in Tumultuous Time of Polarization
    35 / U.S. Department of Education ("US DOE") Proposed Priorities - American History and Civics Education

38 / PART 3 / Grant of Authority to Colorado Board of Education and School Districts; Legislation regarding Academic Standards and Graduation Guidelines

    38 / Colorado Constitution Grant of Authority to Colorado Board of Education and School Districts
    38 / Colorado Legislation Requiring CO DOE to Adopt Academic Standards (CRS § 22-2-106, State Board - Duties – Rules)

39 / Standards in Colorado Legislative Enactments
40 / Colorado Legislation Requiring CO DOE to Adopt Graduation Guidelines (CRS § 22-2-106, State Board - Duties – Rules)

42 / PART 4 / History of § 22-1-104; 48 Years Ago, Colorado Legislature Mandated Public School Instruction about Spanish Americans and Negroes; 25 Years Ago, American Indians Added; 18 Years Ago, Legislature Mandated Satisfactory Completion of Civil Government Course for High School Graduation Starting in 2007, including History, Culture and Social Contributions of African-Americans, Hispanics and American Indians

43 / Colorado House Bill 19-1192: Codified as § 22-1-104, C.R.S.
44 / History, Culture, Social Contributions and Civil Commission Made High School Civics Standards Recommendations in June 2021
45 / School District to Hold Community Forum
45 / Amendment of § 22-1-104 to Detail Civics Instructional Requirements
46 / CO DOE to Assist School Districts in Developing and Promoting Programs
46 / Colorado School Districts and § 22-1-104—Except for Jeffco, Failure to Require Satisfactory Completion of Civil Government Course for High School Graduation, including History, Culture and Social Contributions of African-Americans, Hispanics and American Indians
47 / Internet Cites Stating § 22-1-104 Is in Force and Effect - Satisfactory Completion of Civil Government Course Required for High School Graduation, including History, Culture and Social Contributions of African-Americans, Hispanics and American Indians

50 / PART 5 / Judicial Review of § 22-1-104

50 / Colorado Attorney General Opinion on § 22-1-104
51 / Colorado Appellate Court Decision on § 22-1-104
51 / Colorado Federal District Court, *Lane v. Owens*, 2003, Cited § 22-1-104 in Dicta as Valid Example of Curriculum Requirement
51 / Colorado Supreme Court Decision regarding Use of Term "Must" by General Assembly (aka State Legislature)

53 / PART 6 / Lack of Current Implementation of § 22-1-104 by Colorado Public School Districts, Except for Jeffco, Failure to Require Satisfactory Completion of Civil Government Course for High School Graduation, including History, Culture and Social Contributions of African-Americans, Hispanics and American Indians

53 / Lack of Current Implementation of § 22-1-104
53 / Poudre School District ("PSD") to Comply with HB 19-1192
54 / PSD Social Studies – In February 2021, PSD Stated It Had Not Yet Started to Update Curriculum to Be More Culturally Inclusive
55 / Jefferson County's School District Board of Education ("Jeffco") Updated Civics Curriculum in February 2020 to Comply with HB 19-1192 and 2020 CO DOE Standards

56 / PART 7 / American Indian Presence and History in Colorado

    56 / American Indian Presence in Colorado
    56 / Denver City Council Land Acknowledgement

58 / PART 8 / Why Is American Indian Education Problematic?

    58 / Troubling Legacy
    58 / Kennedy Report in 1969: Non-Indian Teachers and Children Misunderstand Indian Culture and History
    59 / National Congress of American Indians Report: Erasure from Education Fuels Harmful Biases
    59 / Contemporary Stereotypes Regarding American Indians: Rick Santorum

61 / PART 9 / Harm from Lack of American Indian Curriculum

    61 / U.S. Civil Rights Commission Reports Lack of American Indian Curriculum Can (1) Be Harmful to American Indian Students; (2) Contribute to a Negative Learning Environment; (3) Be Isolating and Limiting; (4) Trigger Bullying; and (5) Result in Negative Stereotypes Across the Board
    62 / Awareness of Need for Relevant American Indian Curricular Instruction
    63 / President Obama's Executive Order 13592: Improving American Indian and Alaska Native Educational Opportunities and Strengthening Tribal Colleges and Universities
    64 / Cultural Imperialism
    66 / Statement of Problem in Pathways to Sovereignty: Biased Educational Inputs Produce Disparate Educational Outcomes Jeopardizing Future of American Indian Students

68 / PART 10 / Racism in Colorado High Schools Harmful to American Indians

    68 / Colorado's Durango 9-R Board of Education's January 2021 Resolution Apologizing for Failure to Provide "Equitable Educational Opportunities"
    69 / Denver Public School ("DPS") District – Personal, Structural and Institutional Racism Issues Affecting All Minority Students, Including American Indians
    69 / Denver Public High School Graduation Requirements - No Reference to § 22-1-104
    69 / Denver East High School
    69 / Denver West High School
    70 / Denver North High School
    70 / Denver South High School
    70 / Backlash of Institutional Racism Being Felt in the American Indian Community

72 / PART 11 / Colorado's Minority Academic Achievement Gap Includes American Indians

    72 / American Indians Entitled to State Public Education
    72 / Staggering Negative Academic Performance of AI/AN Students in Colorado
    72 / CO DOE Press Release, August 2020, Building Cultural Awareness in Support of American Indian/Alaska Native Students
    73 / 2011 Colorado Campaign to Boost American Indian Graduation Rates
    73 / Colorado "Native Groups Urge Education Parity," Indian Country Today Article, Original May 7, 2011, Updated Sep. 13, 2018
    74 / Colorado's Black, Latin and LGBTQ Legislative Caucuses and Education Committee Concerned about Educational Achievement Gaps for Minority Students in Colorado

75 / PART 12 / Colorado High Schools' Disproportionate Disciplinary Sanctions Include American Indians

    75 / American Indian Student Disciplinary Rates in Cherry Creek School District 2017-2020

76 / Office for Civil Rights (OCR) of the U.S. Department of Education ("Department") and Cherry Creek School District 2018 Voluntary Resolution Agreement for Disproportionately Subjecting African American Students to Disciplinary Sanctions, Cherry Creek School District, OCR Case Number: 08-17-1245; Final Reporting to OCR August 31, 2019
77 / School-to-Prison Pipeline
79 / Colorado's Office of the Child's Representative - Legal Representation to Children Involved in Colorado Court System
80 / Colorado School Justice Roundtable Hosted by Colorado Attorney General Philip Weiser
80 / Denver Schools Increase Armed Patrol Unit Officers, Seek Authority to Ticket Students
81 / Colorado's Black Caucus Concerned about Disproportionate Discipline of Minority Students in Colorado

83 / PART 13 / Colorado Academic Standards: History and Development - Evidence Systemic Ethnic Cleansing Effort in High School Education of Everything Indian, Sanctioned under Color of State Law

83 / 1998 Colorado Model Content Standards for Civics
84 / 2009 Colorado Civics Standards for High School
84 / 2013 Colorado's District Sample Curriculum Project
84 / 2020 Colorado Civics Standards for High School: Address Indian History, Culture and Social Contributions by Merely Inserting Word "Tribal" Wherever List of Governmental Entities Occur
86 / State of State Standards for Civics and U.S. History in 2021 - Colorado Receives Grade of 'D'
87 / Consultant Analysis of the Colorado Academic Standards for Social Studies
88 / 2021 CO DOE Standards Review Committee – Social Studies
88 / Culturally Responsive Instruction for Native American Students

91 / PART 14 / Holocaust and Genocide Education in Colorado Public Schools

92 / PART 15 / CO DOE Consistent in Stating § 22-1-104 Requirement; Yet No Compliance with Graduation Requirement Monitored or Mandated – No Satisfactory Completion of Civil Government Course Required to Graduate, Including History, Culture and Social Contributions of American Indians

92 / CO DOE Purpose of Graduation Guidelines
92 / CO DOE Consistency in Citing Required Compliance with § 22-1-104 Entitled to Judicial Deference
93 / CO DOE Cites Mandatory Legislative § 22-1-104 Requirement Repeatedly on Its Public Website: Satisfactory Completion of Civil Government Course Required to Graduate, Including History, Culture and Social Contributions of American Indians
93 / CO DOE Monitors School District Compliance with Graduation Guidelines Under an Honor System

96 / PART 16 / CCSD's BOE References Civil Government Graduation Requirement Under § 22-1-104 in Its Graduation Requirements Policy, Yet No Satisfactory Completion of Civil Government Course, Including History, Culture and Social Contributions of American Indians, Actually Required to Graduate

96 / CCSD's BOE References to § 22-1-104 Date Back to 1996
98 / CCSD's Administration Has Confirmed Obligatory Status of § 22-1-104
98 / CCSD's Social Studies Curriculum Does Not Include Civil Government Course, Including History, Culture and Social Contributions of American Indians

100 / PART 17 / CCSD's Curriculum Review with Racial and Cultural Relevance Focus for Kindergarten through Fifth Grade

100 / CCSD's Superintendent Email Message to Parents on April 23, 2021, regarding Curriculum Review with Racial and Cultural Relevance Focus for Kindergarten through Fifth Grade
100 / CCSD's Parents' Respond to Superintendent Siegfried's Email Message to Parents on CCSD Curriculum Review with Racial and Cultural Relevance Focus for Kindergarten through Fifth Grade
101 / Critical Race Theory
101 / CCSD's Media Response to Parents' Concerns at CCSD BOE Meeting regarding Curriculum Review with Racial and Cultural Relevance Focus for Kindergarten through Fifth Grade

103 / PART 18 / CCSD's Social Studies Curricular Resource Review Implementation Scheduled for 2024-2025 - No Mention Whatsoever of § 22-1-104

103 / CCSD's Social Studies Curricular Resource Review Implementation Scheduled for 2024-2025 2025 - No Mention Whatsoever of § 22-1-104
105 / June 23, 2021, CCSD's BOE Meeting: CCSD's Curriculum Review Process
106 / August 9, 2021, CCSD BOE Meeting

111 / PART 19 / CCSD BOE Meeting, September 13, 2021, Minority Academic Achievement Gap, Discipline Statistics for Minorities Continue to Demonstrate Pattern of Disparate Impact – Include American Indians

    111 / CCSD BOE/ District Leadership Team Study Session, Sep. 10, 2021 – Focus on Minority Academic Achievement Gap
    112 / CCSD BOE Study Session, 5 PM, September 13, 2021– Focus on Safety Due to Past Presence of Militia and Unruly Public
    112 / CCSD BOE Meeting, September 13, 2021, 7 PM – Focus on Minority Academic Achievement Gap, Discipline Statistics for Minorities Continue to Demonstrate Pattern of Disparate Impact
    113 / CCSD BOE Meeting, September 13, 2021, Carol Harvey's Public Comment
    114 / Media Coverage of September 13, 2021, Meeting, Especially CCSD's Attempts to Close Academic Achievement Gap for Students of Color
    115 / CCSD BOE Limits Public Comment to People with Connections to District

117 / PART 20 / CCSD's Office of Inclusive Excellence ("OIE") Partnerships for Academically Successful Students ("P.A.S.S.") Indigenous Parent Action Committee ("IPAC") Meetings – Indigenous Parents Had Petitioned CCSD for American Indian Curriculum for Over a Decade

    117 / CCSD's Office of Inclusive Excellence ("OIE") Partnerships for Academically Successful Students (P.A.S.S.) September 16, 2020 Goals
    117 / P.A.S.S. IPAC Meetings
    117 / October 27, 2020, IPAC Public Meeting
    117 / November 18, 2020, IPAC Public Meeting - No Enforcement Component to § 22-1-104; It Had "No Teeth"
    119 / November 19, 2020, IPAC Member Letter to Superintendent re Compliance with § 22-1-104; Letter re Community Forum
    119 / November 19, 2020, IPAC Member CORA Request to CCSD
    120 / December 5, 2020, CCSD's OIE Willing to Discuss § 22-1-104 with IPAC Member

120 / December 8, 2020, IPAC Public Meeting
120 / December 10, 2020, CCSD's CORA Response to IPAC Member
121 / January 12, 2021, IPAC Public Meeting
121 / February 10, 2021, IPAC Public Meeting
122 / February 17, 2021, IPAC Public Meeting
123 / August 26, 2021, IPAC Meeting, ESSER Funds
123 / March 26, 2021, IPAC Member Second CORA Request
124 / March 31, 2021, CCSD - No Timeframe in § 22-1-104 for Compliance
124 / April 2, 2021, CCSD's Second CORA Response – Ten Links to Web Sites
125 / May 2021, IPAC Member Meeting with CCSD

127 / PART 21 / Colorado Education Associations and CCSD Lobbying

127 / Colorado Education Association ("CEA") Supports C.R.S. § § 22-1-104 (1)-(6) (aka HB 19-1192)
127 / Colorado Association of School Boards ("CASB") Legal Opinion – Not Clear § 22-1-104 Constitutional
128 / CASB's Policy on Graduation Requirements - Recommended Language for CO School Districts that Best Meets Intent of Law, includes § 22-1-104(2) Civics Course
128 / CASB, Colorado Association of School Executives ("CASE") and ("CEA") Joint Influence over Legislature and CO DOE
129 / CCSD Lobbying

130 / PART 22 / Colorado High School Diplomas; No Satisfactory Completion of Civil Government Course Required to Graduate, Including History, Culture and Social Contributions of American Indians

130 / Academic Degrees Certify Students' Achievement
130 / Colorado's Tainted Diplomas - No Satisfactory Completion of Civil Government Course Required to Graduate, Including History, Culture and Social Contributions of American Indians
131 / Revocation of Diplomas
131 / Loss of Accreditation for Failure to Comply with Statutory and Regulatory Requirements

132 / PART 23 / Federal Education Funding to State of Colorado for American Indian Students

133 / United States Department of Education ("US DOE") Must Investigate Use of Federal Funding Given to Colorado for American Indian Students
135 / Example of Need for US DOE Audit
136 / U.S. Department of the Interior, Office of Natural Resources Revenue ("ONNR")

138 / PART 24 / Investigation of Colorado Public School Districts, including Cherry Creek School District, to Determine if There Is a Countenanced, Systemic Violation by High Schools of § 22-1-104, C.R.S. - No Satisfactory Completion of Civil Government Course Required to Graduate, Including History, Culture and Social Contributions of American Indians

138 / Petition for Investigation of Colorado Public School Districts, including Cherry Creek School District, to Determine if There Is a Countenanced, Systemic Violation by High Schools of § 22-1-104, C.R.S.
142 / Protest Commenced August 19, 2021 No Satisfactory Completion of Civil Government Course Required to Graduate, Including History, Culture and Social Contributions of American Indians
143 / New Mexico Federal Case - *Yazzie-Martinez v. State of New Mexico*: State's Public Education Department Failed to Provide Native American, Hispanic and Other Students from Diverse Populations a Sufficient Education Due in Part to Lack of Culturally and Linguistically Relevant Curriculum
144 / Email from Governor Polis, September 16, 2021 – No Response on § 22-1-104

145 / PART 25 / Brief Review of Indian History Policy

145 / Stereotypical View of Indians Expressed at Highest Levels of Government
146 / Extermination, Extinction or Starvation for Indians
146 / Annual Report of the Commissioner of Indian Affairs, Nov. 26, 1855: Indians Would Either Be Exterminated by Whites or Become Extinct
147 / Annual Report of the Commissioner of Indian Affairs, Nov. 6, 1858: Allow Indians to Starve or Exterminate Them
147 / Annual Report of the Commissioner of Indian Affairs, Nov. 1859: Gold Discoveries in Colorado; United States Deprived Indians of Any

Means of Subsistence in Colorado
147 / Annual Report of the Commissioner of Indian Affairs, 1862, Commissioner William P. Dole: Colorado and Washington Gold Rushes Infringing on Indian Rights
148 / Annual Report of the Commissioner of Indian Affairs, Oct. 1863: Colorado Territory - Rich in Mineral Wealth; Ute Cession to United States of Arable Land and Mining Districts in Colorado
148 / Annual Report of the Commissioner of Indian Affairs, 1864, Colorado Superintendency: Cheyennes and Arapahoes Want Peace - Military Says Further Chastisement Needed; Sand Creek Massacre
149 / Annual Report of the Commissioner of Indian Affairs, 1865: Metals Are Sole Reliance to Liquidate Interest on National Debt; Cost-Benefit Analysis of Total Destruction of Indians; Whip Cheyennes; Major Wyncoop with Chiefs of Tribes Under His Charge Met with Governor Evans, Colorado, Seeking Peace; Arapahoe and Cheyenne Indians who Escaped from Sand Creek Massacre - Left Almost Helpless in Dead of Winter; Treaty with Arapahoes - No Money, No Specific Land; Commissioners Negotiating with Arapahoes for Treaty – Hard, Mean-Spirited, Sharp Negotiating Tactics Used by U.S., Give Land with Game and Arable Land, Not Gold and Silver
154 / Annual Report of the Commissioner of Indian Affairs, 1866: Treaty with Utes – Gold, Silver and Coal Discovered on Their Land; Fertile Land, Timber, Water Power, All Requirements for Profitable Occupation; Limit Payment to Utes
154 / Annual Report of the Commissioner of Indian Affairs, 1877: Proposal to Remove Indians in Colorado and Arizona to Facilitate Gold and Silver Mining and Farming by Whites
156 / Relocation Program Effect on Colorado

159 / PART 26 / American Indian Education

159 / 2021 Federal Indian Boarding School Initiative
159 / Conversion to Christianity and Education Seen as Solution
160 / Annual Report of the Commissioner of Indian Affairs, 1877: Kill the Indian in Him and Save the Man
161 / Annual Report of the Commissioner of Indian Affairs, 1887: Progress toward Civilization includes Education
162 / Annual Report of the Commissioner of Indian Affairs, 1894: Education to Convert Indians into American Citizens; Education Should Seek Disintegration of Tribes; Inculcate U.S. Patriotism; Indians to Attend Public Schools
163 / Annual Report of the Commissioner of Indian Affairs, 1899:

Education Turned from Tepee, Chase and Barbaric Savage Life to Civilization
164 / Annual Report of the Commissioner of Indian Affairs, 1901: Get Students by Cajolery, Threats, Bribery, Fraud, Persuasion or Force
165 / Meriam Report, 1928, Boarding Schools Inadequate

167 / PART 27 / Conclusion - No Satisfactory Completion of Civil Government Course Required to Graduate, Including History, Culture and Social Contributions of American Indians

167 / *Native News Online* Article, August 27, 2021 - No Comment by Governor; CO DOE – We Don't Audit for Compliance; CCSD - "While Indigenous History Is Definitely Taught In Numerous High School Social Studies Courses, *I Cannot Speak To The Consistency And Depth In Each Relevant Course."*
168 / Pall of Orthodoxy v. Academic Freedom
168 / Obligatory Status of § 22-1-104 - Satisfactory Completion of Civil Government Course Required to Graduate, Including History, Culture and Social Contributions of American Indians
168 / Action Required to Ensure Compliance with § 22-1-104 – Satisfactory Completion of Civil Government Course in Order to Graduate, Including History, Culture and Social Contributions of American Indians
170 / Federal Government Assistance Needed in Colorado - (1) Enforcement of § 22-1-104 which May Be Ignored based on Minority Protected Classes Intended to Benefit from § 22-1-104, Violating Constitutional Rights to Life, Liberty and Property (e.g., Valid Diploma); (2) Investigation of CCSD's Institutional Racism's Impact on CCSD "Consistent, Pervasive and Predictable" Minority Academic Achievement Gap; and (3) Investigation of CCSD's Institutional Racism's Impact on Discipline Statistics for Minorities which Continue to Demonstrate Pattern of Disparate Impact, Including American Indians, Notwithstanding CCSD-OCR Resolution Agreement of 2018
171 / Anarchy in Colorado's Public School System

172 / PART 28 / Post-Script - No Satisfactory Completion of Civil Government Course Required to Graduate, Including History, Culture and Social Contributions of American Indians; Minority Achievement Gap, Including American Indians; Disparate Discipline of Minorities, Including American Indians

172 / Native American Holocaust Honor Song
173 / Native American Holocaust in Colorado's Public High Schools

174 / Addendum

174 / Colorado Students Aren't Supposed To Graduate Without Learning About Indigenous History And Culture Are They? By Jenny Brundin, September 30, 2021.

179 / President Biden's Executive Order on the White House Initiative on Advancing Educational Equity, Excellence, and Economic Opportunity for Native Americans and Strengthening Tribal Colleges and Universities, Oct. 11, 2021.

181 / Non-Verbal Behavior of American Indian Students May Be Used against Them.

183 / 1890 – Colorado Not Happy With Southern Ute Indians Wants Them Gone Too, Report of the Commissioner of Indian Affairs to the Secretary of the Interior, United States. Office of Indian Affairs, U.S. Government Printing Office, 1891, p. XLIV.

184 / Comments Carol Harvey, Resident Cherry Creek School District, Colorado, Colorado Department Of Education, Standards Review Committee – Social Studies.

184 / Colorado Springs Diversity Program Paused.

Acknowledgments

Family:
Nobody has been more helpful to me in the pursuit of this project than the members of my family. They provided emotional support and made sure that whatever resources and assistance I needed for this project were available. Thank you to my most beloved husband (who made breakfast, lunch and dinner and took over all daily family responsibilities so I could focus on this project) whose love provides such joy and stability in my life.

For the Truth Tellers:
Representative Evans' motivation in The Debates and Proceedings in the Congress of the United States on the Indian Removal Act:
If I could stand up between the weak, the friendless, the deserted, and the strong arm of oppression, and successfully vindicate their rights, and shield them in their hour of adversity, I should have achieved honor enough to satisfy even an exorbitant ambition; and I should leave it as a legacy to my children, more valuable than uncounted gold—more honorable than imperial power.
—Representative Evans, speaking on S. 102, on May 18, 1830, 21st Cong., 1st sess., Register of Debates in Congress 1049.

PART 1 / Introduction

High school curriculum equity issues are a hot topic in Colorado. The Cherry Creek School District ("CCSD") Board of Education ("CCSD BOE") meeting on June 23, 2021, evidences the importance of this issue. Almost two hundred people attended the meeting to discuss curriculum revision – the Board meeting room was filled to capacity; an overflow room was opened and it was filled to capacity with people sitting on the floor. More people were outside of the facility watching the meeting online. About a dozen men from an extremist militia group stood guard at the entryway to the meeting, armed with, at a minimum visually, pepper spray. "United American Defense Force ("UADF") is led by former Marine and Benghazi security contractor John "Tig" Tiegen. ... In addition to weapons, UADF provides "access to legal protection for members in the event of having to discharge a weapon to stop a threat."[1]

In a June 22, 2021, email to supporters, FEC United, a conservative group urged them to get involved in school board meetings to oppose everything from critical race theory ("CRT") to mask mandates and vaccination requirements. "Locally, parents continue to rally and fight against CRT in our schools," the email reads. "This week, three of Colorado's school districts have board meetings, which means an opportunity for parents to speak out," it continued before directing members to the Cherry Creek meeting.[2]

Their placard "PARENTS UNITE" identified "The topic for public comment: "CRT and gender identity curriculum. Also, unmasking our kids." They prepared to meet in advance of the CCSD BOE meeting at 6:30 PM to "organize and pray for the meeting, the board members and our kids."[3]

Over one hundred people registered to speak at the meeting, where they were each allotted three minutes. The meeting went on into the early morning of June 24, 2021. An overwhelming majority of the one hundred speakers at the meeting were in support of a culturally responsive curriculum for all students. There were others at the meeting who argued that it is a part of critical race theory.

The CCSD BOE clearly stated in the meeting that Cherry Creek Schools have not and are not adopting the Critical Race Theory. According to Cherry Creek district officials, Critical Race Theory is a theoretical framework, not a curriculum.

After the meeting, Cherry Creek Education Association president and middle school science teacher Kasey Ellis said:

> "We want to thank the Cherry Creek School District for their continued work on equity within the district and look forward to continuing to work with them on this. No matter our color, background or zip code, we want our kids to have an education that imparts honesty about who we are, integrity in how we treat others, and courage to do what's right. But there are those who are now stoking fears about our schools, trying to dictate what teachers say and block kids from learning our shared stories of confronting injustice to build a more perfect union. They push for outdated and inaccurate lessons, redlining the realities of our history in order to justify the harms of our present. What a good teacher knows is we can't just avoid or lie our way through our challenges; we must find age-appropriate ways to tell hard truths about our country's past and present in order to prepare our kids to create a better future."[4]

What led to this significant meeting on June 23, 2021, was one Indian parent's (hereinafter "Indian Parent") pursuit of justice for all minority students.

The subsequent meeting on August 9, 2021, continued the discussion of the need for an inclusive curriculum and compliance with § 22-1-104, C.R.S., as well as opposition to it:

> Max Gimelshteyn, a father of two, said, "I'm here to voice the concerns of hundreds of parents that were not able to get on the list to speak tonight. ... The assertion that the school is simply trying to teach history better is frankly disingenuous and I think anybody doing it is probably aware of that... The so-called cultural response education that is being implemented in K through 12 education often violates the First Amendment and civil rights because it is not being taught as a theory, which would normally require a subject to be analyzed, scrutinized and debate. Instead, it's being practiced as ideology, attempting to coerce children into a certain belief system. It violates First Amendment rights because our government cannot compel...students to profess political, religious or ideological beliefs."

> Jamie Logan, a CCSD teacher and a parent, said ... "We love your kids.

We love every student. ... I promise you that I haven't been spending all summer creating this evil plan to indoctrinate your child with self-loathing and hatred. ... These claims are laughable. ... It's not what we do." She continued, "Please respect my profession. You teach your kids values in your home and I get to teach your kids to be critical thinkers, ask questions, be curious, collaborate. ... We will be talking about race in school. It's really hard. I get it."[5]

NOTES:

1. Far Right Militia Apparently Attends CO School Board Meeting On Critical Race Theory https://coloradotimesrecorder.com/2021/07/far-right-militia-apparently-attends-co-school-board-meeting-on-critical-race-theory/37813/ (accessed online September 5, 2021).

2. Ibid.

3. Ibid.

4. https://kdvr.com/news/local/cherry-creek-schools-hotly-debates-critical-race-theory-how-history-should-be-taught/ (accessed online July 5, 2021).

5. Public Speaks Its Mind At Cherry Creek School Board Meeting, Again, August 18, 2021, Freda Miklin https://villagerpublishing.com/public-speaks-its-mind-at-cherry-creek-school-board-meeting-again/ (accessed online August 25, 2021).

PART 2 / Community Concerns with Non-Inclusive Curriculum, Including American Indians

Indigenous Community Concerned with CCSD's Non-Inclusive Curriculum

Starting in October 2020, the Indigenous Parent Action Committee ("IPAC") within the CCSD publicly addressed the need for the CCSD to comply with § 22-1-104. In 2003, the legislature mandated that students must satisfactorily complete a course on the civil government of the United States and the state of Colorado, as a condition of high school graduation, which expressly included the history and culture of certain minorities, effective with the graduating class of 2007 (SB 36, enacted 4/22/2003).[4] The minorities included African-Americans, American Indians and Latinos.

IPAC had been petitioning the CCSD for the past decade for a curriculum addressing American Indians, with no success. IPAC is comprised of indigenous parents/guardians and staff. IPAC meets monthly and as delineated by the CCSD focuses on the following:

> Illuminating the presence of CCSD's Indigenous community
>
> Amplifying the voices of the Indigenous community by working directly with district leaders to make changes necessary to better serve Indigenous students and families
>
> Forming cross-district partnerships to strengthen the Indigenous community network
>
> Naming the continuous problems of practice embedded in the CCSD learning experience interfering with Indigenous students' academic and social-emotional success (i.e. problematic curriculum resources, erroneous representation and/or lack thereof, microaggressions, normalized harmful traditions/practices i.e. Halloween, Thanksgiving)

Affirming and honoring Indigenous students' presence and cultural identities.[1]

This issue is pertinent in three other states: Montana, New Mexico and South Dakota:

1. Lawsuit Filed Against Montana Violating Constitutional Mandate to Teach Indian Education

https://www.aclu.org/press-releases/lawsuit-filed-against-montana-violating-constitutional-mandate-teach-indian-education

2. Tribal Leaders Demand Action on Public Education Inequity in New Mexico (Including Implementing Culturally Relevant Curriculum)

https://www.santafenewmexican.com/news/education/tribal-leaders-demand-action-on-public-education-inequity-in-new-mexico/article_e00ced8a-f0b7-11eb-a181-cbb3869db7a8.html

3. South Dakota: Native History Gutted in School Curriculum

https://www.indianz.com/News/2021/08/16/harold-frazier-native-history-gutted-in-school-curriculum/

CCSD's Students' Concerned with CCSD's Non-Inclusive Curriculum[2]

In a March 9, 2021, article in the Grandview High School Chronicle, a discussion on curriculum revealed the effort needed for a more inclusive curriculum. I have redacted the names of individuals.

> One group can only stay silent for so long in oppression before they rise up against their oppressors. An event we have seen play out thousands of times throughout history. One of which is now occurring within Grandview.
>
> "There are just a ton of issues in all departments," said senior, _____.
>
> Student representatives relied on both personal experiences and general stories to recall the negative impact of the curriculum on minorities. "Like in history, it is mainly the white community being represented," said

While some representation may be present for minority groups, it is usually only in a negative light.

"I think that just across the board, and in all classes, like other black people... most minorities just struggle," said senior, _____.

Not only is the white representation disproportionate to that of minorities, but some groups are not being accurately portrayed in their modern existence.

"I am Native American, and with my experience it has been that you learn about Native Americans as kind of a historic group of people," said senior, _____. "There is no representation that we exist as normal people today."

When minorities are represented in history classes, it is mostly through the hardships that those groups faced.

"I just feel especially in social studies classes, minorities are only represented as being through struggles, or only going through hardships," said _____.

It goes beyond just the errors in outdated history textbooks and teachings.

"In English, you know the curriculum is especially being talked about because [of] the kind of books and materials that are still being used," said _____. "Like Huckleberry Finn, that's a giant one."

Other minority groups, such as the LGBTQ+ community, are simply asking for even the slightest bit of representation within the school's curriculum.

"I am a gay man and I have never heard a single mention of queer history in any class that I have ever been in, said junior, _____. "Queer history is very important to gender relations specially [sic], so I think that does need better of a focus."

After the students voiced their concerns, the teachers responded with their own changes that they want to make in the classroom to make the curriculum more inclusive.

"I am trying to incorporate more voices just in general that are not white," said CP and AP World History teacher, _____.

Students also cited their own experiences of positive representation in the classroom.

"I have had both _____ and _____, and I think I have seen both of them make efforts towards actually changing their books," said _____. "They did actually remove Huckleberry Finn."

_____ also agreed.

"I can say for _____'s class, last year I definitely saw the effort," said _____. "If she didn't know something as far as what was appropriate, how to address people, she would literally ask us."

The World Language Department also commented on their own changes to incorporate more culture into their lessons.

"In all our level 4 classes, we focus more on culture, and linguistic differences between countries and dialects," said Spanish teacher, _____.

Multiple teachers also commented on their own personal bias, and their wish to continue to expand the amount of perspectives that they include in the classroom.

"I think that there is this bias that we have, this mindset that we have," said_____. "So, I feel as a teacher, I know I am definitely not there yet, but I am really trying to embrace those other perspectives." Business teacher, _____ also commented on his own personal experience from his time in school.

"I can just tell you from personal experience as a person of color, it was life changing for me to find out what my people did in history and my true story, not told by other people, but by our people," said _____. "It was really helpful to me as a human being."

While the teachers want to continue incorporating more minority representation in their courses, they must also grapple with their own fears.

"Getting into these more diverse waters is going to have a lot [sic] white pushback, and a lot of white cis pushback," said _____. "That is something that we have to be brave enough to do."

Teachers also advocated students to be vocal about their concerns.

"Our role as teachers is not to be the sage on the stage, our role is to continue to learn," said _____. "You have a great deal to teach all of us."

Students then voiced their concerns, speaking with a teacher either privately or in a group setting about their concerns with minority representation.

"I just find it is a lot more comfortable going straight to the teacher cause you don't want to deal with other people's judgements about what you are thinking," said _____.

The students also acknowledged how, even though the change to the curriculum will be slow, it is still an active occurrence. "We are not going to be able to change these curriculums overnight," said _____. "[It is important] how we teach the things that we have to at this point, cause these are the things we can see move a little bit right now."

As the meeting drew to a close and the topics were reviewed, one simple message radiated through the entire body of student representatives.

"We have been catering to the white, cis community in our district for so long," said _____.

As the conversation finished, an overwhelmingly positive agreement came over all that were in attendance.

We still have a long way to go in order to represent minorities positively in the school curriculum, a change that cannot occur without the help from everyone.

Grandview must unite on this issue, as it is the only way to take steps towards making everyone feel heard, seen, and represented positively within these walls.

Denver Public School's Black Students Concerned with Non-Inclusive Curriculum

Denver's Black students are also demanding redesign of the Denver Public Schools curriculum to ensure their history is taught. As reported on July 3, 2020, a student led podcast will start with the focus on the experiences of Black Americans.

> The students are also setting their sights on disrupting DPS in a way that will better prioritize Black students and the history of those who came before them. Alliance members have attended multiple meetings with the Denver school board, advocating for the need to change the district's history curriculum so that it better incorporates Black history.[3]

In response to the students push for a more inclusive curriculum, the Denver School Board stated the following:

> Denver school board members announced their intention to pass a resolution to add the "comprehensive historical and contemporary contributions of Black, Indigenous, and Latino communities" to the curriculum from kindergarten to 12th grade. It's a process that's already underway in Denver Public Schools, in part because district leaders recognize the need and in part because students and educators have repeatedly and publicly pointed out the shortcomings of curriculum taught through a white, European lens.[4]

The sad omission is that the Denver Public School District and the CO DOE are not telling students that they don't have to wait on a resolution – there is already a statutory requirement which is being ignored with no negative consequences.

Colorado Senator Rhonda Fields spoke in favor of HB 19-1192 and stated on Twitter: "I have value and that needs to be reflected in our history books."[5]

Other Minorities Concerned with CCSD's Non-Inclusive Curriculum

Other minorities also begin expressing their dissatisfaction with the CCSD's non-inclusive curriculum. A snowball effect was underway.

African-American Community Concerned with CCSD's Non-Inclusive Curriculum

At the April 12, 2021, meeting of the CCSD BOE, an African-American parent accused her daughter's school in the CCSD of "infecting our children with racism." Her daughter's class was given a "slave test," which was graded. Questions included which slaves performing different jobs had the hardest life and what was an overseer's main job? One of the multiple choice answers was "to evaluate the price of slaves."

She continued:

> "We have a serious problem. You have been infecting our children with racism, colorism, white supremacy, white privilege. Not only did you teach this, you graded it. You're not going to keep selling lies. You should be ashamed. ... We have knees on our neck and an education system that let this fall through the cracks. ... At least $40 million goes to pay for the education system here in the state of Colorado."[6]

Brian McKinney, a black father of two CCSD students, questioned why discussions about race were being termed divisive, saying, in part:

> "Do we think it's divisive to our indigenous folks to teach curriculum that says that Europeans discovered this land? Do we think it's divisive to minimize the impacts of slavery, the cruelty of slavery?" He added, "CRT is not being taught in this district, it's not even being taught in this country to K-12. They know it's not being taught. The only reason they are talking about CRT is to stop all equity work in this district. ... Let's talk about race. ... Let's talk about how only 19 percent of black eighth graders are proficient in math. We're dedicated to excellence? Whose excellence are we dedicated to?"[7]

Asian-American Community Concerned with CCSD's Non-Inclusive Curriculum[8]

At the same meeting, Colleen Chan, founder of the CCSD Asian American Pacific Islander (AAPI) task force, joined in the debate for a more inclusive curriculum due to recent racial incidents against Asian-Americans:

> There is an urgent need for immediate implementation of Asian American history in our social studies curriculum. ... History textbooks often define whose experiences and perspectives are necessary, legitimate, and significant in telling the story of the United States. ... What is included in the curriculum sends a message to students. ... For far too long, Asians have been virtually erased from American history...thereby excluding us from being part of this national identity. In grades four, eight, and ten, we teach Colorado state history, but (it) leaves out Denver's Hop Alley (Denver's original Chinatown near 20th and Blake Streets, once home to approximately 1,400 Chinese immigrants, razed in 1940 and replaced with warehouses and industrial buildings), the critical contribution of Chinese

miners and railroad workers, without whom the west would have never been developed.

Chan emphasized the importance of instituting curriculum changes this summer.

Latin Community Concerned with Need for More Inclusive Curriculum Statewide

Colorado Rep. Bri Buentello, D-Pueblo, noted:

> "I think it's about time ... that the whole history is taught to our children," Buentello said during the House floor debate in March. "I think when we teach history in Colorado, we should be talking about all the characters, all aspects and the whole story."[9]

> "Our intent was to start teaching the history of everybody," Colorado Rep. Brianna Buentello, who co-sponsored the bill alongside Rep. Serena Gonzales-Gutierrez, told Reuters. "It's a very different story that's being told than the one, as minorities, we live every single day."[10]

Colorado State Senator Angela Williams stated:

> "Educating our students on the contributions of a number of people from different backgrounds isn't a rewrite of history, its a correction," Colorado State Sen. Angela Williams tweeted on Thursday as the bill was being debated. "I'm proud to speak to the powerful belief that diversity is the source of our strength. Thanks to @SenadoraJuliue for bringing HB19-1192." State Sen. Julie Gonzales introduced the Senate version of the bill.[11]

LGBTQ Community Concerned with Need for More Inclusive Curriculum Statewide

Colorado Rep. Herod is an active supporter of all her constituents, including the LGBTQ community which is many times silently and callously dismissed.

Rep. Leslie Herod stated:

> I support HB 19-1192, Inclusion of American Minorities in Teaching Civil Government, because too often, American Minorities are left out of or tokenized in our educational curriculums.

> Being inclusive does not mean you're excluding. It means that we teach our students about the accomplishments and contributions of all cultures, especially those that have been underrepresented and misrepresented in history books for generations.[12]

Site after Site on the Internet Proclaim Colorado Law Mandating LGBTQ Inclusion in Curriculum

California became the first state to pass a law requiring schools to teach LGBT history in 2011, followed by Colorado and New Jersey in 2019. Civil rights and advocacy groups have praised these states for expanding their definitions of American history in the classroom. "Our youth deserve to see how diverse American history truly is—and how they can be a part of it one day, too," said Christian Fuscarino, executive director of the advocacy group Garden State Equality.[13]

White Community Divided Over Need for More Inclusive Curriculum, CCSD BOE Meeting, June 23, 2021

> A parent pointed out, "It can be hard to talk about (some) facts. Jim Crow is a fact. Segregation is a fact. Housing discrimination, the treaties the United States broke with indigenous nations are facts. ... These are critically important facts that shape and influence what is happening in our country right now. As a **white man**, it can be hard to talk about these facts. ... I'd much rather talk about America saving the day in World War II. I want my kids to think critically about American society so they need to know these facts. Teaching children about the history of redlining that happened right here in our state is not anti-white just like teaching kids about Hitler is not anti-German. It's just reality and this country desperately needs to have a better shared understanding of reality."

> Ashley Andrews saw things differently. Politely and respectively, she said, in part, that, "CRT and the 1619 Project are politically motivated programs and designed to cancel American history and democracy itself. We are fearfully and wonderfully made by our Creator and our nation is based on the understanding that all men are created equal. I implore you not to implement any of these programs and to do so as the other districts have done around them and throw them out..."[14]

Need for Civics Education in Tumultuous Time of Polarization

In its February 2021 Educating for American Democracy Report prepared by a collegial group, they focused on the need for teaching of civics critical at this juncture in our society: "Our republic is at a crossroads, facing deep partisan and philosophical polarization, while understanding of and trust in America's democratic institutions are dangerously low—especially among younger citizens."[15]

This is even more so with the January 2021 Insurrection, along with the many nation-wide protests over Black Lives Matter as referenced in the Colorado Commissioner of Education's Statement on Race and Equity in Education, dated June 10, 2020.[16]

U.S. Department of Education ("US DOE") Proposed Priorities - American History and Civics Education

The Office of Elementary and Secondary Education, US DOE, recognizing the importance of civics to inner-city and rural schools and schools where minority students constitute the majority of the school populations has proposed a grant program:

> $585 million for state education agencies, which would be awarded by formula and passed on to districts to support civics and history education programs, especially with a lens to closing civics achievement gaps. Priority will be given to grant proposals proposing to serve under-served, inner-city, rural and majority minority school populations.[17]

NOTES:

1. https://www.cherrycreekschools.org/Page/13377 (accessed online March 15, 2021).

2. https://ghschronicle.com/7311/news/curriculum-of-equality/ (accessed online June 15, 2021).

3. Denver's Black students are raising their voices to redesign the curriculum, ensure their history is taught, July 3, 2020, Colorado Sun https://coloradosun.com/2020/07/03/black-students-denver-public-schools-racism-history-education-colorado/ (accessed online July 10, 2021).

4. Ibid.

5. https://twitter.com/SenRhondaFields/status/1121479578189307904 (accessed online July 10, 2021).

6. CCSD Parents Speak Out on Issues of Race and Inclusivity in Curriculum, The Villager, May 20, 2021, Freda Miklin https://villagerpublishing.com/ccsd-parents-speak-out-on-issues-of-race-and-inclusivity-in-curriculum/ (accessed online June 10, 2021).

7. Parents Speak Out To The Cherry Creek School Board https://villagerpublishing.com/parents-speak-out-to-the-cherry-creek-school-board/ (accessed online July 10, 2021).

8. CCSD Parents Speak Out on Issues of Race and Inclusivity in Curriculum, The Villager, May 19, 2021, Freda Miklin https://villagerpublishing.com/ccsd-parents-speak-out-on-issues-of-race-and-inclusivity-in-curriculum/ (accessed online July 10, 2021).

9. https://www.coloradopolitics.com/news/colorado-schools-to-teach-a-far-more-inclusive-version-of-history/article_07619028-8195-11e9-9f1a-63bd85281cbd.html (accessed online March 10, 2021).

10. https://www.bustle.com/p/colorado-votes-to-teach-lgbtq-inclusive-curriculum-to-students-in-public-schools-17300826 (accessed online August 10, 2021).

11. Ibid.

12. https://hi-in.facebook.com/LeslieforColorado/videos/comments-in-support-of-hb-19-1192-inclusion-of-american-minorities-in-teaching-c/2299948380331170/Concerns of General Public (accessed online July 10, 2019).

13. https://www.usnews.com/news/best-states/articles/2019-08-14/states-that-require-schools-to-teach-lgbt-history (accessed online July 10, 2021).

https://newrepublic.com/article/162862/republican-laws-ban-lgbtq-history-education (accessed online July 10, 2021).

https://ny.chalkbeat.org/2021/6/8/22524247/lgbtq-history-curriculum-nyc-schools (accessed online July 10, 2021).

https://www.usatoday.com/story/news/education/2021/03/06/lgbtq-history-equality-education-act-teachers/6648601002/ (accessed online July 10, 2021).

14. Parents Speak Out To The Cherry Creek School Board, July 21, 2021 https://villagerpublishing.com/parents-speak-out-to-the-cherry-creek-school-board/ (accessed online July 30, 2021).

15. https://www.educatingforamericandemocracy.org/the-report/ (accessed online April 10, 2021).

16. https://www.cde.state.co.us/cdecomm/statementraceequityined 6102020 (accessed online July 10, 2020).

17. https://www.federalregister.gov/documents/2021/04/19/2021-08068/proposed-priorities-american-history-and-civics-education (accessed online September 5, 2021).

PART 3 / Grant of Authority to Colorado Board of Education and School Districts; Legislation regarding Academic Standards and Graduation Guidelines

Colorado Constitution Grant of Authority to Colorado Board of Education and School Districts

Under the Colorado Constitution, the general supervision of the public schools of the state is vested in the CO DOE. Individual school districts have been created with their own boards of education and the directors of these school district boards have control of instruction in the public schools of their respective districts.

> Section 1. SUPERVISION OF SCHOOLS - BOARD OF EDUCATION
>
> (1) The general supervision of the public schools of the state shall be vested in a board of education whose powers and duties shall be as now or hereafter prescribed by law.
>
> Section 15. SCHOOL DISTRICTS - BOARD OF EDUCATION
>
> The general assembly shall, by law, provide for organization of school districts of convenient size, in each of which shall be established a board of education, to consist of three or more directors to be elected by the qualified electors of the district. Said directors shall have control of instruction in the public schools of their respective districts.[1]

Colorado Legislation Requiring CO DOE to Adopt Academic Standards (CRS § 22-2-106, State Board - Duties – Rules)[2]

The Colorado legislature passed legislation requiring the CO DOE to adopt academic standards in 1993. House Bill 93-1313 required the CO DOE to create standards in reading, writing, mathematics, science, history, civics, geography, economics, art, music and physical education.

The CO DOE explained the purpose of academic standards as follows:

Why standards?

State standards for student learning define what students should know and be able to do at the end of a grade level or grade span. Standards advance equity of outcomes for students by setting a bar for student performance, defining the floor but not the ceiling of student learning.

Standards in Colorado Legislative Enactments

The Colorado state legislature requires standards to be developed under the legislation for standards related to mental health, computer science, Holocaust and Genocide Studies and the civics legislation added by SB 21-067:

22-7-1005 CRS CO DOE Preschool through elementary and secondary education - aligned standards - adoption – revisions (1) On or before December 15, 2009, the state board shall adopt standards that identify the knowledge and skills that a student should acquire as the student progresses from preschool through elementary and secondary education.

(2.3) On or before July 1, 2020, the state board shall adopt standards … related to mental health, including suicide prevention.

(2.5) On or before July 1, 2018, the state board shall adopt standards related to computer science.

(2.7) (a) On or before July 1, 2021, the state board shall adopt standards related to Holocaust and genocide studies. It also requires each school district board of education and charter school to incorporate the standards on Holocaust and Genocide Studies adopted by the state board into an existing course that is currently a condition of high school graduation for school years beginning on or after July 1, 2022. (Emphasis added.)

SB 21-067:

> As soon as is practicable after the effective date of this subsection, the state board of education shall review the **civics portion** of the **social studies standards** and **revise them as necessary** to comply with the requirements of subsection (1)(b) of this section. The state board of education shall **take into consideration any recommendations** of the history, culture, social contributions, and civil government in education commission established in section 22-1-104.3 in reviewing the civics standards pursuant to this subsection (1)(c). (Emphasis added.)

New Statute § 22-7-1005, C.R.S. Requires CO DOE to Revise Social Sciences Standards on or before July 1, 2022

The legislative statute § 22-7-1005 is not a mandate imposed pursuant to §§ 22-1-104 (1-6); it is a revisionary cyclical statutory requirement. Specific standards pertaining to mental health, computer science and holocaust and genocide studies are required. As noted in the statute, the CO DOE is required to take into consideration any recommendations provided by the HB 19-1192 Commission.

22-7-1005 CRS CO DOE Preschool through elementary and secondary education - aligned standards - adoption – revisions (1) On or before December 15, 2009, the state board shall adopt standards that identify the knowledge and skills that a student should acquire as the student progresses from preschool through elementary and secondary education.

> **(2.3)** On or before July 1, 2020, the state board shall adopt standards ... related to mental health, including suicide prevention.
>
> **(2.5)** On or before July 1, 2018, the state board shall adopt standards related to computer science.
>
> **(2.7)** (a) On or before July 1, 2021, the state board shall adopt standards related to Holocaust and genocide studies. In adopting revisions to the standards related to history and civics, the state board shall take into consideration any recommendations provided by the history, culture, social contributions, and civil government in education commission established in section 22-1-104.3.

Colorado Legislation Requiring CO DOE to Adopt Graduation Guidelines (CRS § 22-2-106, State Board - Duties – Rules)[3]

The Colorado legislature passed legislation (§ 22-2-106) requiring the CO DOE to adopt graduation guidelines to better prepare students for either college or a career post-graduation. The legislature recognized that many students needed to be prepared for a post-high school work force, as not all students planned to attend college.

> Local school boards (aka "LEP," "Local Education Provider") may use their own locally-developed graduation requirements so long as they "meet or exceed" any minimum standards or core competencies/skills adopted by the state board.

NOTES:

1. Legislature Supervision of CO BOE

Colorado Constitution, Article 9, Sections 1 and 15
2. https://www.cde.state.co.us/standardsandinstruction/cas-historyanddevelopment (accessed online July 10, 2021).

3. https://www.cde.state.co.us/postsecondary/gradguidelinesfaqs (accessed online July 10, 2021).

PART 4 / History of § 22-1-104; 48 Years Ago, Colorado Legislature Mandated Public School Instruction about Spanish Americans and Negroes; 25 Years Ago, American Indians Added; 18 Years Ago, Legislature Mandated Satisfactory Completion of Civil Government Course for High School Graduation Starting in 2007, including History, Culture and Social Contributions of African-Americans, Hispanics and American Indians

In 1973, the Colorado state legislature enacted §123-21-4, C.R.S, requiring public schools to teach about the history and culture of Spanish-Americans and American Negroes.[1]

While legislation was introduced in 1992 in an attempt to make it optional, it failed to pass (SB 108).[2]

In 1998, it was amended to include American Indians at the urging of Comanche State Representative Suzanne Williams (HB 98-1186, enacted 4/17/1998).[3] Fast-forward twenty-three years and the Indian community has yet to see former Representative and Senator Williams' state legislative lobbying effort to get HB 98-1186 passed being fulfilled.

In 2003, the legislature mandated that students must satisfactorily complete a course on the civil government of the United States and the state of Colorado, as a condition of high school graduation, which expressly included the history and culture of certain minorities, effective with the graduating class of 2007 (SB 36, enacted 4/22/2003).[4] The minorities included African-Americans, American Indians and Latinos.

In May 2019, teaching regarding Asian Americans and the lesbian, gay, bisexual and transgender individuals within these minority groups and the contributions and persecution of religious minorities were added to the statute (HB 19-1192, enacted 5/28/2019).[5]

On April 29, 2021, it was further amended by SB 21-067 to address specific topics under federal and state constitutions and governments.[6]

Colorado House Bill 19-1192: Codified as § 22-1-104, C.R.S.

On May 28, 2019, Colorado House Bill 19-1192 ("HB 19-1192") (codified as § 22-1-104, C.R.S.) was passed by the Colorado state legislature, addressing the need for an inclusive curriculum in the state's public schools. **It specifically became effective immediately**. It provides as follows:

22-1-104. Teaching of history, culture, and civil government.

> The history and civil government of the United States and of the state of Colorado, which includes the history, culture, and social contributions of minorities, including, but not limited to, American Indians, Latinos, African Americans, and Asian Americans, the lesbian, gay, bisexual, and transgender individuals within these minority groups, and the intersectionality of significant social and cultural features within these communities, and the contributions and persecution of religious minorities, must be taught in all the public schools of the state.

HB 19-1192 was introduced by Rep. Gonzales-Gutierrez, a granddaughter of Denver activist Rudolfo "Corky" Gonzales, a leader in the Crusade for Justice group. While a senior at Denver's West High School in 1969, Rep. Gonzales-Gutierrez's mother participated in protests on March 20-21, 1969. One grievance was the lack of Chicano curriculum. Students from Manuel, Thomas Jefferson, Lincoln and South High Schools, all came out and supported the students at West High School. The protests came to be known as the "blowouts." Numerous arrests occurred in what the demonstrators had hoped would be a non-violent presentation of their grievances to school administrators.

As reported by CPR News,

> The West blowouts helped kick-start what became known as El Movimiento, the Chicano Movement. Just a few weeks later, the Crusade for Justice held the first ever Youth Liberation Conference. Nearly 1,500 young Chicanos from across the country were drawn to Denver.[7]

In a symbolic ceremony, Governor Jared Polis signed HB 19-1192 at Denver's Rudolfo "Corky" Gonzales Branch Library. Rep. Gonzales-Gutierrez stated: "Our diversity is what makes our country and our state strong, but for too long, individuals and communities that have moved or immigrated here and those that have been here for many centuries ... have been excluded from our teaching of history." Three generations later, one Latinx family seeking an inclusive curriculum has yet to see the fruition of its activism.[8]

History, Culture, Social Contributions and Civil Commission Made High School Civics Standards Recommendations in June 2021

A 16-member History, Culture, Social Contributions and Civil Commission was established under § 22-1-104.3 **to make recommendations** to the state board of education and department of education to be used in conjunction with the regular six-year review of the state's education standards and programs pursuant to § 22-7-1005(6). In June 2021, they submitted their recommendations to the CO DOE.[9] It is important to note that recommendations do not have to be accepted. It is in the CO DOE and a school's sole discretion to reject any or all of them.

> Section 22-1-104.3 - History, culture, social contributions, and civil government in education commission - established - membership – duties
>
> **(1)** There is established the history, culture, social contributions, and civil government in education commission, referred to in this section as the "commission". The purpose of the commission is to make recommendations to the state board of education and department of education to be used in conjunction with the regular six-year review of the state's education standards and programs pursuant to section 22-7-1005(6). The recommendations must seek to further the discovery, interpretation, and learning of the history, culture, social contributions, and civil government of the United States and Colorado, including the contributions of American Indians, Latinos, African Americans, and Asian Americans, the lesbian, gay, bisexual, and transgender individuals within these minority groups, and the intersectionality of significant social and cultural features within these communities, and the contributions and persecution of religious minorities. The commission shall work cooperatively and in conjunction with the department of education and local school boards of education as described in section 22-1-104.

(2) The commission consists of sixteen members and, to the extent practicable, must include persons from throughout the state and persons with disabilities and must reflect the ethnic diversity of the state. A majority of the commission members must have either classroom experience or experience in developing education content standards.

(4) Beginning in September 2019, the commission shall meet a minimum of two times per year and additionally as needed in conjunction with the community forums established in section 22-1-104(3)(a).

School District to Hold Community Forum

Each school district is also required to hold a community forum to discuss adopted content standards in civics, including, but not limited to, the contributions of American Indians, Latinos, African Americans, and Asian Americans, the lesbian, gay, bisexual and transgender individuals within these minority groups, and the intersectionality of significant social and cultural features within these communities, and the contributions and persecution of religious minorities.

(3)(a) In an effort to increase civic participation among young people, each school district board of education shall convene a community forum on a periodic basis, but not less than once every six years, for all interested persons to discuss adopted content standards in civics, including the subjects described in subsection (1) of this section. The history, culture, social contributions, and civil government in education commission established in section 22-1-104.3 shall actively participate in any such forums. **(b)** Based upon input from this community forum, each school district board of education shall determine how the subject areas specified in subsection (1) of this section are addressed when establishing graduation requirements.

Amendment of § 22-1-104 to Detail Civics Instructional Requirements

With the amendment of § 22-1-104, C.R.S., by Senate Bill 21-067 on April 29, 2021, signed by Governor Polis, schools will have to focus on the instruction and discussion of the fundamentals of American democracy at the federal, state and local levels, and include classroom activities where students model democratic processes. It requires the CO DOE to develop standards and includes a very short timeline for compliance.

CO DOE to Assist School Districts in Developing and Promoting Programs

The CO DOE is tasked with **assisting school districts in developing and promoting programs** for § 22-1-104. **Programs are defined as activities or projects.**

> (4)(a) In an effort to strengthen the teaching of the history, culture, social contributions, and civil government of the state of Colorado and of the United States in all public schools of the state in accordance with the requirements of this section, the department of education, in conjunction with the history, culture, social contributions, and civil government in education commission established in section 22-1-104.3, shall assist the school districts of the state in developing and promoting programs for elementary and secondary students that engage the students in the process of discovery and interpretation of the subjects and topics set forth in subsection (1) of this section.

Colorado School Districts and § 22-1-104 – Except for Jeffco, Failure to Require Satisfactory Completion of Civil Government Course for High School Graduation, including History, Culture and Social Contributions of African-Americans, Hispanics and American Indians

In researching school districts in Colorado, there is not much discussion regarding § 22-1-104. It is uncertain how many, if any, Colorado school districts have a civil government course complying with § 22-1-104. A Google search only turned up the Cherry Creek, Jefferson County and the Poudre School Districts. It would seem Jefferson County is the only district that is in compliance with § 22-1-104.[10] Also, even though the state legislature in 2003 made the completion of a course including these subjects a condition of graduation, school districts are willfully ignoring § 22-1-104. Students receive diplomas even if they have not been offered or satisfactorily completed the course required under § 22-1-104.

The Colorado Early Colleges Board of Directors has established the following graduation requirements for all students pursuing graduation. All of the following criteria must be met in order for a student to graduate:

> *Social Science credit includes the satisfactory completion of a civics/government course that encompasses information on both the United States and State of Colorado (C.R.S 22-1-104).[11]

Internet Cites Stating § 22-1-104 Is in Force and Effect - Satisfactory Completion of Civil Government Course Required for High School Graduation, including History, Culture and Social Contributions of African-Americans, Hispanics and American Indians

Various internet cites state § 22-1-104 is in force and effect in Colorado when this is false. It raises a question regarding the integrity of the state and deceptive advertising.[12]

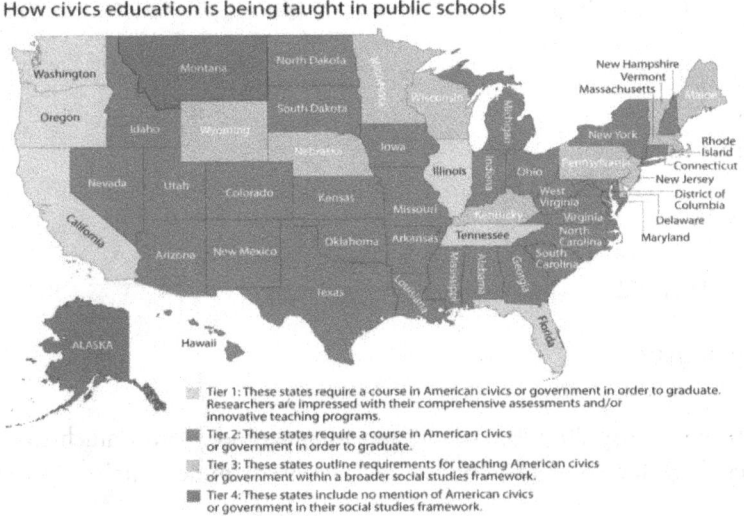

https://www.csmonitor.com/Media/Content/2018/0323/0323-civics-map

> "Colorado in particular has one of the most robust civics education requirements in the country. In fact, the only statewide graduation requirement in Colorado is the completion of a civics and government course. Colorado designed curriculum for a full year civics course, and provides a myriad of resources and guidance for teachers on the subject." https://populationeducation.org/an-essential-guide-to-civics-education-in-the-united-states-today/

Education Commission of the States

> Colorado: Public schools are required to teach a course on the history and civil government of the state of Colorado and the United States, to include the history, culture and contributions of minorities. Satisfactory completion of this course is required for high school graduation. C.R.S. 22-1-104[13]

NOTES:

1. §123-21-4, C.R.S, 1973

2. 1992 SB 108

3. 1998 HB 1186

4. 2003 SB 36

5. 2019 HB 19-1192

6. 2021 SB 21-067

7. https://www.cpr.org/2019/03/18/chicano-progress-today-owes-much-to-the-denver-west-high-blowouts-of-50-years-ago/ (accessed online March 1, 2021).

8. www.coloradopolitics.com/news/colorado-schools-to-teach-a-far-more-inclusive-version-of-history/article_07619028-8195-11e9-9f1a-63bd85281cbd.html (accessed online March 5, 2021).

9. https://www.cde.state.co.us/standardsandinstruction/1192commission (accessed online August 20, 2021).

10. https://www.thepulsefromcandi.com/blog/category/socialstudies (accessed online August 20, 2021).

11. https://coloradoearlycolleges.org/wp-content/uploads/CEC_Files/CEC_Fort_Collins/Documents_Forms/FC_HS_and_Westminster/Graduation_Requirements_FC.pdf (accessed online January 5, 2021).

12. https://www.csmonitor.com/Media/Content/2018/0323/0323-civics-

map (accessed online March 5, 2021).
https://populationeducation.org/an-essential-guide-to-civics-education-in-the-united-states-today/ (accessed online March 5, 2021).
https://www.americanprogress.org/issues/education-k-12/reports/2018/02/21/446857/state-civics-education/ (accessed online March 5, 2021).
https://www.aft.org/ae/summer2018/shapiro_brown (accessed online March 5, 2021).
https://medium.com/generation-citizen/mapping-the-civic-education-policy-landscape-9e5766692efe (accessed online March 5, 2021).
https://www.edweek.org/teaching-learning/data-most-states-require-history-but-not-civics (accessed online March 5, 2021).

13. https://ecs.secure.force.com/mbdata/MBQuest2RTANW?Rep=CIP1601S (accessed online March 5, 2021).

PART 5 / Judicial Review of § 22-1-104

Colorado Attorney General Opinion on § 22-1-104

The Colorado Attorney General has upheld § 22-1-104 as follows:

> "Generally the legislature has authorized local school district boards of education "to determine the educational programs to be carried on in the schools of the district . . . ." C.R.S. 1973, 22-32-109(1)(t). However, the legislature presently mandates certain minimum requirements as to what must be taught, including the history and civil government of the state and of the United States, C.R.S. 1973, 22-1-104, honor and use of the United States flag, C.R.S. 1973, 22-1-06, United States Constitution, C.R.S. 1973, 22-1-108, and the effects of the use of alcohol, C.R.S. 1973, 22-1-110 (Supp. 1982)."

> "I conclude that a state has authority to impose academic and nonacademic requirements as a condition of promotion at various levels of K-12 education and/or as a condition of receiving a high school diploma, as long as constitutional rights of due process and equal protection are observed."[1]

See 1983 CO Attorney General Opinion State Legislature Has Authority to Impose Academic Graduation Requirements, including § 22-1-104, 983 Colo. AG LEXIS 33 (Dec. 2, 1983).

See Comment: The Colorado Charter Schools Act and the Potential for Unconstitutional Applications Under Article IX, Section 15 of the State Constitution, 67 U. Colo. L. Rev. 171, Winter, 1996, FN 47.

Colorado Appellate Court Decision on § 22-1-104

More importantly, a Colorado appellate court also upheld § 22-1-104 as follows:

> The board of education has been given statutory authority to "determine the educational programs to be carried on in the schools of the district." Section 22-32-109(1)(t), C.R.S. (1988 Repl. Vol. 9). However, the board's discretion is not unlimited, and the General Assembly has specified certain subjects that must be taught. These subjects are: the history, culture, and civil government of Colorado and the United States, including the history, culture, and contributions of minorities, *see* § 22-1-104, C.R.S. (1988 Repl. Vol. 9); honor and use of the flag, *see* § 22-1-106, C.R.S. (1988 Repl. Vol. 9); the federal constitution, *see* § 22-1-108, C.R.S. (1988 Repl. Vol. 9); and the effect of alcohol and controlled substances. *See* § 22-1-110, C.R.S. (1988 Repl. Vol. 9).[2]

See *Skipworth v. Board of Educ.*, 874 P. Ed. 487 (1994).

Colorado Federal District Court, *Lane v. Owens*, 2003, Cited § 22-1-104 in Dicta as Valid Example of Curriculum Requirement

A federal district court cited § 22-1-104 in dicta as an example of a valid curriculum requirement versus the rote recitation of the Pledge of Allegiance. See *Lane v. Owens*, U.S. District Court of Colorado, Civil Docket Case No 1:03-cv-01544-LTB, Judge Lewis T. Babcock, August 15, 2003, Ruling (pp. 6-7). Plaintiffs were successful in their Preliminary Injunction petition. Defendants included the CCSD, Adams-Arapahoe (Aurora), Denver County 1, and Jefferson County R-1 (Jeffco) Public School Districts.[3]

Colorado Supreme Court Decision regarding Use of Term "Must" by General Assembly (aka State Legislature)

Also, according to the Colorado Supreme Court, the Colorado General Assembly's use of the term "must" "connotes a mandatory requirement." See *Waddell v. People*, 462 P.3d 1100, 1106 (Colo. 2020), citing *Ryan Ranch Cmty. Ass'n v. Kelley*, 380 P.3d 137, 146 (Colo. 2016).

NOTES:

1. 1983 CO Attorney General Opinion State Legislature Has Authority to Impose Academic Graduation Requirements, including § 22-1-104, 983 Colo. AG LEXIS 33 (Dec. 2, 1983).

Comment: The Colorado Charter Schools Act and the Potential for Unconstitutional Applications Under Article IX, Section 15 of the State Constitution, 67 U. Colo. L. Rev. 171, Winter, 1996, FN 47.

2. *Skipworth v. Board of Educ.*, 874 P. Ed. 487 (1994).

3. *Lane v. Owens*, U.S. District Court of Colorado, Civil Docket Case No 1:03-cv-01544-LTB, Judge Lewis T. Babcock, August 15, 2003, Ruling (pp. 6-7).

PART 6 / Lack of Current Implementation of § 22-1-104 by Colorado Public School Districts, Except for Jeffco - Failure to Require Satisfactory Completion of Civil Government Course for High School Graduation, including History, Culture and Social Contributions of African-Americans, Hispanics and American Indians

Lack of Current Implementation of § 22-1-104

> Even with the long history of § 22-1-104 going back to 1993, judiciary support and its predecessor statute going back to 1977, the implementation of the instruction and graduation requirement is wholly uncertain. Many Colorado school districts find themselves in the same position as that found by the Poudre School District and the CCSD, with no course compliant with § 22-1-104.

Poudre School District ("PSD") to Comply with HB 19-1192

The PSD has been under extra public scrutiny due to minority community concerns. In February 2021, the PSD added language to its Social Studies webpage that it will follow all mandated curricula set forth in approved legislation from the Colorado General Assembly and signed by the Governor, including HB 19-1192. However, in its Equity Report under Curriculum and Assessment, it noted that it had not started an effort to include culturally relevant content. It is uncertain how this is to be interpreted as no additional information was provided to the public.

PSD Social Studies – In February 2021, PSD Stated It Had Not Yet Started to Update Curriculum to Be More Culturally Inclusive

Social Studies Education in PSD

> The Colorado Academic Standards for Social Studies focus on academic skills. In high school, we provide a number of courses and pathways to teach these skills, however, there are some common elements that all PSD students can expect to encounter in Social Studies. Poudre School District will follow all mandated curricula set forth in approved legislation from the Colorado General Assembly and signed by the Governor. This currently includes HB 19-1192 Inclusion of American Minorities In Teaching Civil Government. This was signed into law by Governor Jared Polis in 2020 and mandates instruction in public schools of history and civil government of the United States and Colorado, including but not limited to the history, culture, and social contributions of American Indians, Latinos, African Americans, and Asian Americans; lesbian, gay, bisexual, and transgender individuals within these minority groups; the intersectionality of significant social and cultural features within these communities; and the contributions and persecution of religious minorities.[1]

However, the PSD, in its February 10, 2021, District Update on Equity, Diversity and Inclusion, informed its constituency that it had not yet started to update its curriculum to be more culturally inclusive. Specifically, it stated the following in regard to Curriculum and Assessment:

Ensure culturally inclusive content

> Review and revise current curriculum adoption process to include culturally inclusive content (not started)

> Develop culturally inclusive and responsive rubrics so staff can reflect on current content, assessments, and practices (not started).[2]

Jefferson County's School District Board of Education ("Jeffco") Updated Civics Curriculum in February 2020 to Comply with HB 19-1192 and 2020 CO DOE Standards

Jeffco updated its Civics Units of Study in February 2020 to comply with § 22-1-104 and CDE's 2020 Standards.[3]

NOTES:

1. https://www.psdschools.org/department/social-studies (accessed online June 8, 2021).

2. https://www.psdschools.org/news/february-equity-diversity-update (accessed online June 8, 2021).

3. https://www.thepulsefromcandi.com/blog/category/socialstudies (accessed online August 8, 2021).

PART 7 / American Indian Presence and History in Colorado

American Indian Presence in Colorado

Compliance with § 22-1-104 by Colorado school districts is important to American Indians due to the large American Indian population in Colorado. Colorado was the traditional territory of Ute, Cheyenne and Arapaho peoples and forty-eight contemporary Indian Nations have historical ties to Colorado as well. These forty-eight contemporary Indian Nations lived or hunted in Colorado and have many sacred sites in the state. For example, two of the four sacred mountains of the Navajo people which they considered as the northern and eastern boundaries of their homelands are located in southern Colorado— Mt. Blanca and Mt. Hesperus.

Also, there are two federally recognized Indian Nations in the southwest corner of the state- the Southern Ute Nation near Durango, Colorado, and the Ute Mountain Ute Nation near Cortez, Colorado.

Further, the federal government chose Denver in 1952 for the headquarters of its relocation program. The program moved American Indians from reservations to urban areas for the purpose of their assimilation and to provide employment and educational opportunities. Denver was a popular choice for relocatees and many that came here under the relocation program stayed in Colorado and made it home.

Denver City Council Land Acknowledgement

The Denver City Council Land Acknowledgement reflects the importance of Indian history, culture and social contributions to the state and the past and present "exclusions and erasures of Indigenous Peoples:"

The Denver City Council honors and acknowledges that the land on which we reside is the traditional territory of the Ute, Cheyenne, and Arapaho Peoples. We also recognize the 48 contemporary tribal nations that are historically tied to the lands that make up the state of Colorado.

We honor Elders past, present, and future, and those who have stewarded this land throughout generations. We also recognize that government, academic and cultural institutions were founded upon and continue to enact exclusions and erasures of Indigenous Peoples.

May this acknowledgement demonstrate a commitment to working to dismantle ongoing legacies of oppression and inequities and recognize the current and future contributions of Indigenous communities in Denver.[1]

NOTES:

1. https://www.denvergov.org/Government/Departments/Denver-City-Council/About (accessed online April 8, 2021).

PART 8 / Why Is American Indian Education Problematic?

Troubling Legacy

The topic of education is still troubling today to American Indians. Education was seen as a mechanism for the 'absorption of tribes and extinguishment of reservations' by assimilating them. This is signified by the famous 1892 quote: 'kill the Indian in him, and save the man.'[1] It was hoped that American Indians would cease to exist as a distinct people, merging with the white communities engulfing them. Yet many American Indians refused to give up their individual tribal identities and cultures. Their refusal was costly—they dropped out of the punitive education systems they encountered. Others, longing for acceptance, chose affirmation and approval, relinquishing their Indian identities.

American Indian tribes ceded over a billion acres of land and tribes were assured in return that the federal government would deliver educational services, medical care, and technical and agricultural training

Kennedy Report in 1969: Non-Indian Teachers and Children Misunderstand Indian Culture and History

In 1969, the Committee on Indian Education submitted a discouraging report entitled *Indian Education: A National Tragedy-A National Challenge*, also known as the Kennedy Report. The report claimed that one of the main problems with public school education for American Indian children was that non-Indian teachers and children misunderstood Indian culture and history. We have not advanced far beyond this.

National Congress of American Indians Report: Erasure from Education Fuels Harmful Biases

The National Congress of American Indians ("NCAI"), the largest and most representative national organization serving the interests of Indian Nations, commissioned a nation-wide study of public school education regarding American Indians, including Colorado. The 2016-2018 Reclaiming Native Truth (RNT) project found that the invisibility of Native peoples is pervasive and entrenched across all sectors of American society.

It concluded as follows:

> The invisibility of Native peoples and the erasure of contemporary Native Americans' contributions, innovations, and accomplishments in K-12 education fuels harmful biases in generation after generation of Americans who grow up learning a false, distorted narrative about Native Americans. In most schools, information about Native peoples is either completely absent from the classroom or relegated to brief mentions, negative information, antiquated references, or inaccurate stereotypes. According to the RNT research, teaching students accurate Native history is not enough to break through the invisibility and stereotypes that feed and perpetuate bias and racism; it is also imperative to teach about contemporary Native issues and the accomplishments of Native peoples today.[2]

NCAI's purpose for issuing the Report was for it to "serve as a platform to build momentum, engagement and support for a movement to transform K-12 education to accurately represent Native peoples' cultures, histories, diversity, contributions, and contemporary place in today's society."

Contemporary Stereotypes Regarding American Indians: Rick Santorum

In April 2021, former U.S. Senator Rick Santorum stated that there was "nothing here" before European settlers arrived. His comment exposes the grave need for Indian curriculum.

> "We came here and created a blank slate," Santorum said. "We birthed a nation from nothing. I mean, there was nothing here. I mean, yes we have Native Americans, but candidly there isn't much Native American culture in American culture."[3]

Fawn Sharp, president of the NCAI, countered his statement with the fact that European colonizers found "thousands of complex, sophisticated, and sovereign Tribal Nations, each with millennia of distinct cultural, spiritual and technological development."[4]

He ended up losing his position as a CNN commentator.

NOTES:

1. Official Report of the Nineteenth Annual Conference of Charities and Correction (1892), 46–59. Reprinted in Richard H. Pratt, "The Advantages of Mingling Indians with Whites," Americanizing the American Indians: Writings by the "Friends of the Indian" 1880–1900 (Cambridge, Mass.: Harvard University Press, 1973), 260–71.
https://upstanderproject.org/firstlight/pratt (accessed online January 5, 2021).

2. Reclaiming Native Truth (2018). Research Findings: Compilation of All Research. Echo Hawk Consulting & First Nations Development Institute, June 2018.

3. https://www.usatoday.com/story/entertainment/tv/2021/04/26/rick-santorum-dismisses-native-american-culture-spurring-backlash/7384340002/ (accessed online April 30, 2021).

4. https://www.ncai.org/news/articles/2021/04/26/ncai-president-fawn-sharp-s-statement-re-rick-santorum-comments-to-young-american-foundation (accessed online April 30, 2021).

PART 9 / Harm from Lack of American Indian Curriculum

U.S. Civil Rights Commission Reports Lack of American Indian Curriculum Can (1) Be Harmful to American Indian Students; (2) Contribute to a Negative Learning Environment; (3) Be Isolating and Limiting; (4) Trigger Bullying; and (5) Result in Negative Stereotypes Across the Board

The U.S. Civil Rights Commission in its December 2018 Report "Broken Promises: Continuing Federal Funding Shortfall for Native Americans" found that "Today, the vast majority of Native American students attend public schools operated by state and local authorities."[1]

They determined that:

> In addition, for Native American students learning in schools without historically accurate representation or discussion of Native American people in curriculum, the educational experience can be isolating and limiting. The lack of accurate and culturally inclusive curriculum on Native Americans also limits the ability of all students to understand and be aware of the history and contributions of Native Americans.[2]

The same is true for all minorities.

Specifically:

A lack of appropriate cultural awareness in school curriculum focusing on Native American history or culture also raises concerns. …

/ 61

The White House Initiative on American Indian and Alaska Native Education heard concerns that curricula surrounding Native American history or culture may be irrelevant or inaccurate, and may sometimes use inappropriate Native American clothing, songs, dances, customs, and arts, which can potentially have harmful effects on Native American students. Moreover, the White House Initiative on American Indian and Alaska Native Education found that this can contribute to a negative learning environment, as Native students may be confronted with misinformation that they may feel compelled to correct, which can cause uncomfortable and difficult situations, and can possibly trigger bullying.

Recent national public opinion polling also shows that lack of accurate history about Native Americans in U.S. public education may contribute to negative stereotypes across the board.[3]

The U.S. Civil Rights Commission recommended "grant funding to develop curricula and lesson guides that state and local school districts may then choose to adopt to maximize instruction that includes non-derogatory, culturally inclusive discussion of Native American history and student experience."[4]

Awareness of Need for Relevant American Indian Curricular Instruction

The tragic situation confronting American Indian students is compounded by the length of time the U.S. government has known of the importance of Indian curriculum (e.g., Meriam Report in 1928).

In 2009, W. Journell, wrote the article, "An incomplete history: Representation of American Indians in State Social Studies," analyzing difficulties with the representation of American Indians in social studies classes:

> Nowhere do definitions of the traditional curriculum resonate louder than with the depiction of American Indians and Alaska Natives in public school classrooms. Studies have shown that students enter public education conceptualizing American Indians as warlike, half-naked savages, a depiction stemming from cartoons and Hollywood productions. Although the educational process begins to sophisticate students' understanding of American Indians rather quickly, research shows that students' knowledge of American Indian culture plateaus around fifth grade when discussions of American history turn to the American Revolution and the subsequent rise of the American nation (Brophy, 1999). From that point forward, researchers

found that American Indians "disappeared or were mentioned only as faceless impediments to western expansion" (p. 42).[5]

Ogbu (1987, 1992) contends that members of minority groups need to feel as if they are positively represented in curricula in order to become engaged in their education. He argues that this is particularly important for what he terms "involuntary minorities," groups that were either forcibly brought to the United States or systematically oppressed by Europeans, such as African Americans and American Indians. In order for members of those groups to embrace public schooling, they must see examples of people like themselves within the curriculum, which often does not occur with traditional forms of social studies education. Moreover, when members of minority groups are mentioned within the curriculum it is often to remind students of periods in history when a particular group was discriminated against and then to celebrate their subsequent struggle for equality. This practice raises an important question regarding the representation of marginalized groups in American history; should members of minority groups be included within the curriculum as exemplars of people who fought for liberation against their oppressors, or as productive members of society that have contributed to the social, political, and economic fabric of our nation? (Epstein, 1998).[6]

President Obama's Executive Order 13592: Improving American Indian and Alaska Native Educational Opportunities and Strengthening Tribal Colleges and Universities

On December 2, 2011, President Obama signed Executive Order 13592—Improving American Indian and Alaska Native Educational Opportunities and Strengthening Tribal Colleges and Universities, recognizing the unique political and legal relationship the United States has with the federally recognized American Indian and Alaska Native (AI/AN) tribes across the country, as set forth in the Constitution of the United States, treaties, Executive Orders, and court decisions.

> For centuries, the Federal Government's relationship with these tribes has been guided by a trust responsibility a long standing commitment on the part of our Government to protect the unique rights and ensure the well-being of our Nation's tribes, while respecting their tribal sovereignty. In recognition of that special commitment and in fulfillment of the solemn obligations it entails Federal agencies must help improve educational opportunities provided to all AI/AN students, including students

attending public schools in cities and in rural areas. ... This is an urgent need. Recent studies show that AI/AN students are dropping out of school at an alarming rate, that our Nation has made little or no progress in closing the achievement gap between AI/AN students and their non-AI/AN student counterparts, and that many Native languages are on the verge of extinction.[7]

Cultural Imperialism

In 2014, Donna Martinez, PhD, with the University of Colorado at Denver wrote the article, "School Culture and American Indian Educational Outcomes," repeating the educational problems confronting American Indian students in Colorado. While the quotes are lengthy, it is important to capture her analysis.

> American Indian students have the lowest educational attainment rates of any group in the United States. Many American Indian students perceive their current classroom experiences as unrelated to them culturally.[8]

> Insisting that the culture of school is more important than culture of students' homes is a form of cultural imperialism. Educational institutions believe that they offer a "culture blind" education to all American students; an education where race and cultural backgrounds of students do not matter, a reportedly culture-free zone.[9]

> The idea of cultural blindness masks entrenched inequality. Educators assume that racial harmony is the norm in cultureless classrooms. Many view the underperformance of American Indian students in education as merely representing the lack of individual hard work and determination. Current educational disparities are viewed as a reflection of individual underachievement and lack of educational potential.[10]

> A continuing educational gap in access to higher education, in a knowledge-based economy affects the socio-economic status of families and tribes. Many American Indian families depend on public education as a pathway to upward mobility and increased opportunities. Reservations remain economically underdeveloped, and the full potential of many American Indian students, untapped.[11]

> Both Gallup and Kaiser Family polling data indicate that the majority of white Americans believe that racial discrimination no longer exists, that we

live in a post-racial, color-blind, or race neutral society (Gallagher, 2012). The myth of color and cultural blindness maintains white privilege by negating the reality of racial and cultural inequality that American Indians face in American institutions.[12]

A 2012 ASHE report attributes American Indian attrition rates to the lack of representation of American Indians in curriculum and among teachers (McKinney, 2012). A U.S. Department of Education study identified the top reasons why American Indian students drop out of school: (1) *uncaring teachers*, (2) *curriculum* designed for mainstream America, and (3) *tracking* into low achieving classes and groups (Department of Education, 1991).[13]

An analysis of social studies curriculum found that American Indians are largely depicted as victims, rather than recognized for their contributions to American culture (Journell, 2009). Any American Indian history that is covered in schools focuses on a limited time frame of pre-twentieth century history. Contemporary achievements of tribal self-determination are excluded from school curriculums, as well as a substantial pre-Columbian history of ancient civilizations in America. This serves to reinforce media images of American Indians as people who existed in the past. Americans can feel as though they have accepted people who only existed in the past (Willow, 2010). Nearly all states cease their coverage of American Indians after wars in 1860s, creating an incomplete narrative. This creates significant implications for the historical consciousness of all students, and especially for American Indian students.[14]

While some states have passed legislation to support teaching about Americans Indians, no funding to support culturally relevant curriculum changes or teacher training accompany these measures. American Indians have struggled to gain a presence in educational curriculum. In the 1990s, a political "culture war" occurred in the United States regarding the presentation of public school history curriculum. Liberals asserted that a critical reading of national history needed to be presented; while conservatives felt that a celebration of "traditional" American historical accounts should be stressed. National educational standards, developed in 1994, did not expand the presence of American Indians in school curriculum.[15]

The Department of Education Indian Nations at Risk Task Force identified top priorities as the need for culturally and linguistically based education, and the need to train more American Indian teachers (Locke, 2007).[16]

Statement of Problem in Pathways to Sovereignty: Biased Educational Inputs Produce Disparate Educational Outcomes Jeopardizing Future of American Indian Students

"Pathways to Education Sovereignty: Taking a Stand for Native Children Presented by the Tribal Education Alliance, New Mexico," stated the problem with the biased education in public schools is that the schools are absolutely and completely 'resistant to change' and the 'historical injustices' of failures to comply with the law continue unabated, without consequences, except to Indian children who are irreparably harmed.

> Native children have the right to an adequate and sufficient education, but at each stage of their lives the public education system fails them. From early childhood through primary, secondary and post-secondary schooling, the cumulative effect of under-resourced, misguided and—to this day—biased educational inputs produces disparate educational outcomes. This systemic equity gap in education jeopardizes the future of Native students and the future of tribal communities.[17]
>
> Over two years later, the state has yet to make meaningful investments in Native children. It has yet to embrace a shift in attitude and approach. Instead, a pattern of resistance to change emerged.[18]
>
> The continuum of historical injustices, present day failures to comply with laws and court orders, and the prospect of losing future generations to a Western way of life is evident to New Mexico's Nations, Tribes and Pueblos.[19]

This is equally applicable to Colorado.

NOTES:

1. U.S. Civil Rights Commission, December 2018 Report "Broken Promises: Continuing Federal Funding Shortfall for Native Americans, p. 221.

2. Ibid., pp. 221-222.

3. Ibid., p. 121.

4. Ibid., p. 222.

5. Journell, W. (2009). An incomplete history: Representation of American Indians in State Social Studies. *Journal of American Native Indian Education*. *Retrieved from* http://jaie.asu.edu/v48/index.html, p. 20 (accessed online March 1, 2021).

6. Ibid., p. 21.

7. https://obamawhitehouse.archives.gov/the-press-office/2011/12/02/executive-order-13592-improving-american-indian-and-alaska-native-educat (accessed online March 1, 2021).

8. Donna Martinez, "School Culture and American Indian Educational Outcomes," Procedia - Social and Behavioral Sciences 116 (2014), 199. *Retrieved from* https://www.researchgate.net/publication/260758836_School_Culture_and_American_Indian_Educational_Outcomes (accessed online March 1, 2021).

9. Ibid.

10. Ibid., 200.

11. Ibid.

12. Ibid.

13. Ibid., 201.

14. Ibid., 202.

15. Ibid.

16. Ibid.

17. Pathways to Education Sovereignty: Taking a Stand for Native Children Presented by the Tribal Education Alliance, New Mexico, p. 7. https://nabpi.unm.edu/assets/documents/tea-full-report_12-14-20.pdf (accessed online September 5, 2021). See also Native Nations and American Schools: The History of Natives in the American Education System, The National Indian Education Association http://www.niea.org/nieaflipbook/mobile/index.html#p=1 (accessed online September 5, 2021).

18. Ibid.

19. Ibid., p. 14.

PART 10 / Racism in Colorado High Schools Harmful to American Indians

Colorado's Durango 9-R Board of Education's January 2021 Resolution Apologizing for Failure to Provide "Equitable Educational Opportunities"

Colorado's Durango 9-R Board of Education in January 2021 passed a resolution apologizing for what they claim is a failure to identify and address "diversity, equity and inclusion" across the district in a "systemic" way. The resolution further says the district has failed to provide those students "equitable educational opportunities in a safe and healthy environment."[1]

Excerpt from Resolution:

> WHEREAS, the District currently includes culturally diverse students, families, and staff representing many countries and territories, including approximately 21% of students who are Latino, 6% who are American Indian or Alaska Natives, 1% who are African American, and 1% who are Asian;
>
> WHEREAS, the District acknowledges the presence of harmful injustices that extensive research has shown to exist at the intersections of race, class, religion, gender, sexuality, and abilities; and
>
> WHEREAS, the District, despite past efforts, continues to have significant opportunity gaps as evidenced by disproportionate rates of discipline, drop-out, and achievement among various subpopulations;
>
> THEREFORE, BE IT FURTHER RESOLVED, that the Board apologizes to the community, particularly to our students, families, staff, and alumnae, for not yet effectively identifying and addressing diversity, equity, and inclusion across the district in a systemic way ...

Denver Public School ("DPS") District – Personal, Structural and Institutional Racism Issues Affecting All Minority Students, Including American Indians

DPS operates 207 schools, including traditional, magnet, charter and pathways schools, with a current total enrollment of about 92,331 students. Of those, 56% of the school districts enrollment is Hispanic, 23% is Caucasian, 13% is African American, 3% is Asian, 4% is more other, and 1% is American Indian. 140 languages are spoken, and 37% are English language learners. 11% of students have special needs. The poverty rate is 70%.[2]

Many of the school websites acknowledge the local, city, and national context where personal, structural and institutional racism exist and persist; that this reality continues to negatively impact the lives of our students and staff members; and that they are committed to change.

Denver Public High School Graduation Requirements - No Reference to § 22-1-104

The Denver Public High School Graduation Requirements make no mention of § 22-1-104.03[3]

Denver East High School

At Denver East High School, Black Lives Matter.

> Our school, a proudly diverse community of learners, exists in a local, city, and national context where personal, structural and institutional racism exist and persist. We know that this reality continues to negatively impact the lives of our students and staff members. We are committed to examining our beliefs and understandings, dismantling racist structures, and creating anti-racist policies and actions that ensure high levels of success in the learning lives of our black students. This commitment includes the recruitment, hiring, and retention of black educators to teach our Angels with excellence.[4]

Denver West High School

> Our mission is to dismantle systemic racism by cultivating an inclusive

school environment that provides a personalized education to every student with the opportunity to engage in rigorous college and career coursework and experiences. [5]

Denver North High School

North High School catalyzes the academic and personal success of all students, transforming them to reach their full potential at the post-secondary program of their choice and to be leaders in an ever-changing world.[6] There is no reference to racism.

Denver South High School

South is committed to dismantling systemic and structural racism in education, and creating academic access and facilitating success to Black and all Students of Color. Moving forward as a community, we will work to create a diverse, equitable, and inclusive environment for all students to feel supported academically and personally, being empowered to pursue their dreams beyond South. We, Denver South, are committed to being actively anti-racist and building a future we can all prosper in.[7]

Surprisingly, after this statement, a STEM laboratory class photo of all white students is shown.

Backlash of Institutional Racism Being Felt in the American Indian Community

At a Denver Indian organization on September 1, 2021, a grandparent of an American Indian-African-American granddaughter told me that on her granddaughter's first day of AP Social Studies class at North High School in Metro Denver her teacher said he was a racist, working it out after required training, and if any student had any issues with that they were going to have problems. The mother complained to the Principal who, according to her, "swept it under the rug." Students are afraid and have **texted each other** to that effect.

Having been in an employment setting where employees were required to attend 'diversity training,' I am aware firsthand of the **backlash and the resentment of**

white employees. It is important for minority students to be in AP classes. The negative learning environment created by this teacher must be rectified. **A new teacher should be assigned to this class given the mistrust and fear already established.**

NOTES:

1. https://pagetwo.completecolorado.com/2021/07/29/durango-school-board-apologizes-for-racism-cant-point-to-any-instances-of-discrimination/ (accessed online September 6, 2021).

2. https://en.wikipedia.org/wiki/Denver_Public_Schools (accessed online September 2, 2021).

3. https://collegeandcareer.dpsk12.org/wp-content/uploads/sites/33/2019_GraduationRequirements_District_Final.pdf (accessed online September 2, 2021).

4. https://east.dpsk12.org/ (accessed online September 2, 2021).

5. https://dps.schoolmint.net/school-finder/schools/8147/west-high-school (accessed online September 2, 2021).

6. https://north.dpsk12.org/ (accessed online September 2, 2021).

7. https://denversouth.dpsk12.org/ (accessed online September 1, 2021).

PART 11 / Colorado's Minority Academic Achievement Gap Includes American Indians

American Indians Entitled to State Public Education

American Indians are entitled to public school benefits on the same basis as all other state citizens. A limited amount of federal funding is provided to states for the education of American Indian students in Colorado.

Staggering Negative Academic Performance of AI/AN Students in Colorado

Colorado's indigenous community is concerned with the horrific academic performance of its children. Any ethnic group with the benchmarks reported by the CO DOE would generate significant concern. Approximately 81% of AI/AN students in Colorado are not meeting state math benchmarks; approximately 85% of AI/AN students are not meeting state science benchmarks; approximately 70% of AI/AN students are not meeting state English language benchmarks. These are staggering numbers of AI/AN students who are not being adequately educated to succeed in very competitive academic and employment arenas.[1]

CO DOE Press Release, August 2020, Building Cultural Awareness in Support of American Indian/Alaska Native Students

The CO DOE issued a Press Release in August 2020, on Building Cultural Awareness in Support of American Indian/Alaska Native Students.[2] It does not appear much progress has been made.

Assumption #3- Colorado's American Indian history is accurately represented in current curriculum and the American Indian perspective is included for a comprehensive look at historical events. The Indigenous People of Colorado occupied the land thousands of years before the first European settlers arrived. However, much emphasis in schools is placed on the conflicts, battles and wars before, during and after the colonial time period in written history.

2011 Colorado Campaign to Boost American Indian Graduation Rates

In August 2011, the Colorado's Commission of Indian Affairs launched a new campaign to curb high drop-out rates among the state's Native American students.

> State officials know they face a challenge, as according to the most recent state figures, half of all native students in Colorado won't finish high school. Nevertheless, the campaign hopes to build on some earlier Indian education successes in Colorado, such as a law that requires that Native American history be taught in public schools.[3]

Colorado "Native Groups Urge Education Parity," Indian Country Today Article, Original May 7, 2011, Updated Sep. 13, 2018

> Colorado has a law-largely ignored-that dictates the teaching of American Indian culture and history in public schools, but it is an unfunded mandate that most school districts have said they don't have the money to implement, according to concerned parents and community members.
>
> A state statute enacted more than a decade ago requires the schools to teach American Indian "history, culture and contributions" as well as that of other minority groups. and says that satisfactory completion of the subject is a condition of high school graduation.
>
> Given Colorado's 68 percent dropout rate for Indian students, several groups are marshaling forces to attack the public education shortcomings they say undermine the well-being of the Indian community, most of whose members are concentrated along the Rocky Mountain Front Range and in the Denver metro area.

Colorado's Black, Latin and LGBTQ Legislative Caucuses and Education Committee Concerned about Educational Achievement Gaps for Minority Students in Colorado

Colorado's Black, Latin and LGBTQ Legislative Caucuses and Education Committee are all concerned about educational achievement gaps for minority students occurring in Colorado. To investigate this matter, Senators Rodriguez, Buckner, Gonzales, Moreno, Pettersen, Story, Zenzinger and Garcia, along with Representatives Gutierrez, Duran, Amabile, Bacon, Benavidez, Bernett, Caraveo, Cutter, Froelich, Hooton, Jackson, Kennedy, Kipp, McCormick, Ortiz, Sirota, Snyder, Weissman, Woodrow, Young, Boesenecker, Esgar, Exum, Gray, Herod, McLachlan, Michaelson-Jenet, Ricks, Titone, Jodeh and McCluskie introduced legislation for an audit.

A major sponsor of the legislation (HB 21-1294), Senator Robert Rodriguez of Denver, wanted an audit to consider whether aspects of Colorado's education accountability system "maintain institutional or cultural biases." To get the Bill passed, he had to agree to a change in the language to whether "unintended barriers or obstacles" affect the performance of students from different groups. It was signed by Governor Polis on July 2, 2021.[4]

NOTES:

1. www.cde.state.co.us/fedprograms/statereportcard (accessed online February 8, 2021).

2. https://www.cde.state.co.us/fedprograms/building-cultural-awarenessinsupportofamericanindianandalaskanativestudents (accessed online February 8, 2021).

3. https://www.kunc.org/education/2011-08-02/state-effort-looks-to-boost-indian-grad-ra (accessed online February 8, 2021).

4. 19. Changes steer audit of Colorado accountability system away from looking for bias in state tests
https://co.chalkbeat.org/2021/6/4/22519284/colorado-school-ratings-accountability-system-audit-bias (accessed online September 14, 2021); http://leg.colorado.gov/bills/hb21-1294

PART / 12 Colorado High Schools' Disproportionate Disciplinary Sanctions Include American Indians

American Indian Student Disciplinary Rates in Cherry Creek School District 2017-2020[1]

2020-2021: CCSD TOTAL STUDENTS 52,226:
American Indian or Alaska Native Students 0.6%, **297**
2019-2020: TOTAL STUDENTS 53,743:
American Indian or Alaska Native Students 0.6%, **310** *(7.42%)*
2018-2019: TOTAL STUDENTS 53,625
American Indian or Alaska Native Students, 0.6%, **309** *(9.71%)*
2017-2018: TOTAL STUDENTS 53,394
American Indian or Alaska Native Students 0.6%, 302 *(8.94%)*

	YEAR	2017-2018	2018-2019	2019-2020
	NO. OF AI/AN STUDENTS	302	309	310
	% OF STUDENT BODY	0.6%	0.6%	0.6%
	PERCENTAGE DISCIPLINED	8.94%	9.71%	7.42%
	TYPE OF DISCIPLINE			
A	Classroom Removal			
B	In School Suspension	8	12	5
C	Received One Out of School Suspension	9	17	14
D	Received Multiple Out of School Suspension	7	4	3
E	Total Out of School Suspensions	27	30	23
F	Expulsion With Services			
G	Expulsion Without Services			
H	Referrals to Law Enforcement		5	2
I	School Related Arrest			
J	Other Action			
K	Unduplicated Count of Students Disciplined	18	26	20

Office for Civil Rights (OCR) of the U.S. Department of Education ("Department") and Cherry Creek School District 2018 Voluntary Resolution Agreement for Disproportionately Subjecting African American Students to Disciplinary Sanctions, Cherry Creek School District, OCR Case Number: 08-17-1245; Final Reporting to OCR August 31, 2019

The issue of disparate disciplinary practices for students of color is not new to the CCSD. In September 2018, the CCSD entered into a Voluntary Resolution Agreement for Disproportionately Subjecting African American Students to Disciplinary Sanctions, with the Office for Civil Rights (OCR) of the U.S. Department of Education, OCR Case Number: 08-17-1245. Final Reporting under the Voluntary Resolution Agreement to OCR was on August 31, 2019.

> OCR is responsible for enforcing Title VI of the Civil Rights Act of 1964 ("Title VI"), and its implementing regulation, at 34 Code of Federal Regulations (C.F.R.) Part 100, which prohibit discrimination based on race, color, or national origin in programs or activities receiving Federal financial assistance from the Department. As a recipient of Federal financial assistance from the Department, the District is subject to this law and regulation.
>
> The Title VI regulations, at 34 C.F.R. Section 100.3(a) and (b), provide that a school district may not treat individuals differently on the basis of race, color, or national origin with regard to any aspect of the services, benefits, or opportunities it provides.
>
> To determine whether a district has discriminated against a student on the basis of race in the discipline process, OCR looks at: (1) whether there is evidence that the student was treated differently than students of other races under similar circumstances; and (2) whether the treatment has resulted in the denial or limitation of education services, benefits, or opportunities. If there is such evidence, OCR next examines: (1) whether the district provided a nondiscriminatory reason for its actions; and (2) whether there is evidence that the stated reason is a pretext for discrimination. To find a violation, the preponderance of the evidence must establish that the district's actions were based on the student's race.
>
> The Title VI regulations, at 34 C.F.R. Section 100.3(b)(2), provide that a school district may not use criteria or methods of administration which have the effect of subjecting individuals to discrimination because of their race, color, or national origin. To determine whether a district's

disciplinary process has an unlawful disparate impact on the basis of race, OCR examines: (1) whether a discipline policy or practice that is neutral on its face has a disproportionate, adverse effect on students of a particular race; and (2) whether the policy or practice is educationally necessary (i.e., whether there is a substantial, legitimate educational justification); and, if so, (3) whether there is an alternative policy or practice that would result in a lesser disparate impact and be comparably effective in meeting the district's educational objectives.[2]

A complaint alleged that the District's discipline policies and practices discriminate against African American students ("Systemic Allegation"). During the course of investigating the Systemic Allegation ... the District indicated its desire to voluntarily enter into an agreement to resolve the Systemic Allegation pursuant to Section 302 of OCR's Case Processing Manual (CPM).

Data from OCR's Civil Rights Data Collection (CRDC), the District, and the Colorado Department of Education (CDE) indicate that African American students in the District are disproportionately subjected to disciplinary sanctions.

OCR will monitor implementation of this Agreement through periodic reports from the District about the status of the Agreement terms.[3]

School-to-Prison Pipeline

The lack of positive representations of the history, culture and social contributions of students of color also impacts the School-to-Prison pipeline and the impact exclusionary discipline has on students of color, LGBTQ students, and students with disabilities. Of the American Indian students in the CCSD, 8-10% of approximately 300 students over the past three years have experienced suspensions, with the majority out-of-school.[4]

In an April 2021 Report of the Pennsylvania Advisory Committee to the U.S. Commission on Civil Rights, Disparate and Punitive Impact of Exclusionary Practices on Students of Color, Students with Disabilities and LGBTQ Students in Pennsylvania Public Schools A Report of the Pennsylvania Advisory Committee to the U.S. Commission on Civil Rights (April 2021), the Committee found:

> Data show that students of color, students with disabilities, and students who identify or are perceived as lesbian, gay, bisexual, transgender, and/

or queer (LGBTQ) are more likely to face exclusionary school discipline (such as suspensions, expulsions, or disciplinary transfers) and/or contact with law enforcement. These practices place children in the "school-to-prison pipeline", a term which refers to the "collection of policies, practices, conditions, and prevailing consciousness that facilitate both the criminalization within educational environments and the processes by which this criminalization results in the incarceration of youth and young adults." Research has consistently shown that the unequal application of exclusionary discipline is a function of different treatment, not different student behavior.[5]

The adverse effects exclusionary discipline practices have on excluded students, the student's classroom, and the school community are harmful and well-documented. Students who are suspended become at risk for future forms of exclusionary discipline, significant loss of instruction exacerbating any pre-existing academic difficulties, and an increased likelihood of becoming incarcerated. These students are highly susceptible to school discipline due to a lack of culturally competent school policies, often displayed in student codes of conduct, which perpetuate a narrow definition of expected and acceptable student behavior.[6]

Recent research from the U.S. Department of Education's Civil Rights Data Collection (CRDC) combined with achievement data determined that the racial discipline gap was positively correlated with the racial achievement gap. This can be explained by the reality that a suspension from school removes the child from the learning environment, denies access to teachers and instruction, often with little transition support when returning to school. In January 2014 guidance on the nondiscriminatory administration of discipline, the federal government cited the correlation between exclusionary discipline and the "potential for significant, negative educational and long-term outcomes" and reiterated the CRDC's evidence of schools disparately disciplining students of color and students with disabilities. It also reminded school districts that they were engaging in "unlawful discrimination" based on race "if a policy is neutral on its face - meaning that the policy itself does not mention race - and is administered in an evenhanded manner but has a disparate impact, i.e., a disproportionate and unjustified effect on students of a particular race." It is also important to remember the larger school environment when considering disparate discipline; efforts to address disparate discipline will be more effective when schools are simultaneously addressing underlying education inequities.[7]

Keri Smith, a representative of Padres & Jóvenes Unidos, which works with parents and students of color in Denver and other districts, said that for many years, the group's ideas about school discipline reform were not welcome at the Capitol. Their major priority this year—a school discipline overhaul collapsed in the face of fierce opposition from law enforcement and concern from some districts and education groups.

Colorado's Office of the Child's Representative - Legal Representation to Children Involved in Colorado Court System

The Office of the Child's Representative is the state agency charged with providing competent and effective best interests legal representation to children involved in the Colorado court system. It explicitly affirms the disproportionate rate of referral of minorities, including Indigenous and Native students to law enforcement at school.

School to Prison Pipeline and Practice Tips for Advocating Against School Expulsions

> The school to prison pipeline wreaks havoc on our clients by criminalizing conduct part and parcel to being young and by disparately targeting students of color, students with disabilities, and students who identify as LGBTQ. According to the Colorado Division of Criminal Justice, in 2019, 5% of students across our state identified as Black or African American; but 10% of students referred to law-enforcement at school were Black or African American. Students who identified as White constitute 59% of the student body and 52% of the students who were referred to law enforcement at school. Hispanic and Latinx students as well as Indigenous and Native students experienced a similar disproportionate rate of referral to law enforcement at school. Implicit bias and systemic racism at school directly lead to students of color having disproportionate contact with the criminal and delinquency systems for no other reason than race or color.[8]

This article was prepared by Litigation Support List (LST) Member Elie Zwiebel.

Colorado School Justice Roundtable Hosted by Colorado Attorney General Philip Weiser

In a School Justice Roundtable hosted by Colorado Attorney General Philip Weiser, the community discussed disparities in school disciplinary treatment for minorities. The state is aware of the problem and the school to prison pipeline, but unable to find a solution.

> Disparities in school disciplinary treatment are well-documented, especially for Black, Latino/a, Native American, LGBTQ, and students with disabilities. Within many districts, punitive measures, including law enforcement citations and arrests, are meted out to students from these groups at disproportionately high rates. Nationally, Black male students are three times more likely to be suspended or expelled than their peers. In Colorado, data from the 2018-19 academic year shows that Black students composed 5% of the statewide student body, but were subject to 10% of all school-based arrests or citations and 36% of arrests or citations for "public peace" offenses.[9]

Denver Schools Increase Armed Patrol Unit Officers, Seek Authority to Ticket Students

Notwithstanding the concerns minority parents have with the school-to-prison pipeline issue, the Denver Public School system plans to use its armed patrol unit of twenty-five officers to ticket students for certain violations, listed below.

> While the district believes the arrangement furthers its goal of reducing student interactions with police, some advocates see it as a bait-and-switch. Denver Public Schools will no longer have 18 Denver police officers stationed inside schools issuing tickets, but if the arrangement is finalized, the district's expanded mobile force of 25 armed patrol officers would now have that authority. "They're not finding the solution; they're just finding new ways of criminalizing our students," said Elsa Bañuelos, executive director of the advocacy group Padres & Jóvenes Unidos.[10]

> These are the municipal code violations for which Denver Public Schools armed patrol officers could issue tickets:
>
> Possession or consumption of marijuana

Assault
Public fighting
Threats
Trespassing
Destruction of public property
Destruction of private property
Petty theft (of an item valued at less than $2,000)
Possession of injection devices
Possession of prohibited graffiti materials
Carrying, wearing, or using dangerous or deadly weapons
Selling, carrying, or using certain knives
Throwing stones or missiles
Parking in a private driveway
Parking in violation of posted signs.[11]

Colorado's Black Caucus Concerned about Disproportionate Discipline of Minority Students in Colorado

"Black, brown, queer and disabled kids are disproportionately impacted by harsh discipline policies, and we have to change it," said state Rep. Leslie Herod, a Denver Democrat and sponsor of the bill.

Senate Bill 21-1821 seeks to minimize student run-ins with police, boost district reporting of discipline practices and create positive, alternative ways to address student behavior. The bill notes more than 4,000 Colorado students were ticketed or arrested for a nonviolent misdemeanor at schools in the 2017-18 school year. During the 2018-19 academic year, Black students in Colorado were 3.2 times more likely to be suspended than were white students, and Hispanic students were 1.7 times more likely to be suspended than white students. Students with disabilities were three times more likely to be arrested than their non-disabled peers, according to an ACLU study. Research also indicates that suspension and ticketing are not effective deterrents and lead to greater problems.[12]

The Bill was withdrawn due to opposition.

NOTES:

1. https://coloradochildrep.org/school-to-prison-pipeline-and-practice-tips-for-advocating-against-school-expulsions/ (accessed online September 6, 2021).

2. Letter Re Resolution Agreement https://www2.ed.gov/about/offices/list/ocr/docs/investigations/more/08171245-a.pdf (accessed online September 14, 2021).

3. Resolution Agreement https://www2.ed.gov/about/offices/list/ocr/docs/investigations/more/08171245-b.pdf (accessed online September 14, 2021).

4. https://www.cde.state.co.us/cdereval/rvprioryearsdidata (accessed online August 5, 2021).

5. https://www.usccr.gov/files/2021/04-09-Pennsylvania-Public-Schools.pdf, p. 3 (accessed o33nline September 5, 2021).

6. Ibid., p. 2 (accessed online September 5, 2021).

7. Ibid., p. 5 (accessed online September 5, 2021).

8. https://coloradochildrep.org/school-to-prison-pipeline-and-practice-tips-for-advocating-against-school-expulsions/ (accessed online September 6, 2021).

9. School Justice Roundtable: Engaging Our Community A recap of the School Justice Roundtable hosted by Attorney General Philip Weiser, written by Adam Rice and Felicia Schuessler. https://coag.gov/app/uploads/2021/03/School-Justice-Report_Engaging-Our-Community_22021-2.pdf (accessed online September 6, 2021).

10. https://co.chalkbeat.org/2021/9/9/22665809/denver-schools-armed-security-guards-ticket-students (accessed online September 13, 2021).

11. Ibid.

12. https://co.chalkbeat.org/2021/3/12/22328371/colorado-racial-disparities-discipline-bill-school-to-prison-pipeline

PART 13 / Colorado Academic Standards: History and Development - Evidence Systemic Ethnic Cleansing Effort in High School Education of Everything Indian, Sanctioned under Color of State Law

Standards for student learning are not new in Colorado. Passed in **1993**, House Bill 93-1313 initiated standards based education in Colorado. The statute required the state to create standards in reading, writing, mathematics, science, history, civics, geography, economics, art, music and physical education. Local communities and educators choose their own curriculum, which is a detailed plan for day-to-day teaching. Former Arkansas Governor Mike Huckabee once used a football analogy to explain the difference. An example of a standard is the game rule that you need ten yards to gain a first down. Curriculum encompasses all of the options available to the team on offense to achieve that goal.[1]

1998 Colorado Model Content Standards for Civics

Even though § 22-1-104 required teaching about the history, culture and social contributions of Spanish-Americans and American Negroes, there are only two references to American Negro issues. American Indians were added April 17, 1998, so they were not addressed in these Standards, though the statute adding American Indians did not require standards to start teaching about the history, culture and social contributions of American Indian.

Civics, Grades 9-12 As students in grades 9-12 extend their knowledge, what they know and are able to do includes:

> Developing, evaluating, and defending positions about historical and contemporary efforts to act according to constitutional principles (for example, abolition movement, desegregation of schools, civil rights movements) and ...

analyzing, using historical and contemporary examples, the meaning and significance of the idea of equal protection* of laws for all persons (for example, Brown v. Board of Education, University of California v. Bakke)....²

2009 Colorado Civics Standards for High School

No reference to § 22-1-104 or African Americans, American Indians or Hispanics or other terms for these groups, i.e., Native Americans.³ This is confirmed by Connor Kirwan Warner, in his study of state social studies standards for American Indian education, which included Colorado. He found that Colorado does not specify any concrete information that students must learn about living American Indians (Colorado Department of Education, 2009).⁴

2013 Colorado's District Sample Curriculum Project

The 2013 teacher-authored High School, Social Studies Complete Sample Curriculum created during Colorado's District Sample Curriculum Project in 2013 has NO references to American Indians or tribes, Blacks (Africans, Negroes), Hispanics or Latinos or Spanish-Americans. The authors of the Sample were Rachel Nelson (Plateau Valley 50) and Janis Schimmel (Cherry Creek).⁵

2020 Colorado Civics Standards for High School: Address Indian History, Culture and Social Contributions by Merely Inserting Word "Tribal" Wherever List of Governmental Entities Occur

In 2020, the CO DOE promulgated Social Studies Standards and noted that school district compliance with § 22-1-104 is required. These Standards remain in full force and effect until superseded.

> ***Civics as a Graduation Requirement** In 2004, the Colorado State Legislature passed a bill requiring all high school students to pass a course in civics. This is the only state graduation requirement. Specifically, the law states, "Satisfactory completion of a course on the civil government of the United States and the state of Colorado ... shall be a condition of high school graduation in the public schools of this state.*⁶ (Emphasis added).

The Civics Standards addressed Indian history, culture and social contributions by merely inserting the word "tribal" wherever a list of governmental entities occurred:

> Participate in civil society at any of the levels of government, local, state, tribal, national, or international.
>
> Participation in a local, state, tribal, or national issue involves research, planning, and implementing appropriate civic engagement
>
> Civic-minded individuals understand how the U.S. system of government functions at the local, state, tribal, and federal level in respect to separation of powers and checks and balances and their impact on policy.
>
> Assess how members of a civil society can impact public policy on local, state, tribal, national, or international issues. For example: voting, participation in primaries and general elections, and contact with elected officials.
>
> *Nature and Skills of Civics:*
>
> 1. Civic-minded individuals use appropriate deliberative processes in multiple settings, such as caucuses, civic organizations, or advocating for change at the local, state, tribal, national or international levels.
>
> 3. Civic-minded individuals evaluate citizens' and institutions' effectiveness in addressing social and political problems at the local, state, tribal, national, and/or international levels.
>
> 5. Civic-minded individuals analyze how people can use civic organizations, and social networks, including media to challenge local, state, tribal, national, and international laws that address a variety of public issues.
>
> 7. Civic-minded individuals evaluate multiple procedures for making and influencing governmental decisions at the local, state, tribal, national, and international levels in terms of the civic purposes achieved.[7]

State of State Standards for Civics and U.S. History in 2021 - Colorado Receives Grade of 'D'

The Thomas B. Fordham Institute, a renowned research, analysis, and commentator on education, conducted a review of the states' standards for Civics and U.S. History.[8] For Colorado, it reviewed: "Colorado Academic Standards: Social Studies," 2020, https://www.cde.state.co.us/ cosocialstudies/2020cas-ss-p12.

Overview:

Its June 2021 analysis concluded that Colorado's civics and U.S. History standards are inadequate. In general, they fail to specifically reference essential content, and the sporadic lists of persons or events that accompany the broad grade-level expectations don't delineate a proper scope or sequence. A complete revision of the standards is recommended.

>Civics: D
>Content & Rigor: 2/7
>Clarity & Organization: 1/3
>Total Score: 3/10
>U.S. History: D
>Content & Rigor: 2/7
>Clarity & Organization: 1/3
>Total Score: 3/10

Civics

>**Strengths** 1. The content for early grades is generally age appropriate and often quite specific.

>**Weaknesses**

>1. Many standards are too broad and vague to provide useful guidance.
>2. Most essential content is missing at the high school level.
>3. Organization is needlessly complex and confusing.

History

Strengths 1. There is considerable emphasis on history-related analytical and research skills.

Weaknesses

1. Historical content guidance is extremely thin, thematically scattered, and stripped of context.
2. The Colonial era is relegated to grade 5.
3. The complex organizational structure is needlessly confusing and often redundant.

Dr. Amber Northern, Senior Vice President for Research with The Thomas B. Fordham Institute interview with Ross Kaminsky on June 24, 2021, described Colorado's standards as "wishy-washy," "vague and amorphous." "The lack of detail is problematic." It's a "recipe for disaster" in holding students accountable. It's a "travesty" for the children of Colorado. Politically they aren't likely to offend anyone because they don't say anything. Colorado needs to "go back to the drawing board."[9] (Emphasis added).

Consultant Analysis of the Colorado Academic Standards for Social Studies, August 2021

CDE requested assistance in identifying current international, national, and state trends that would inform CDE of the alignment to or gaps among the Colorado Social Studies Standards and the current trends and in addressing any changes to the current standards that may be considered in the future.[10]

This resulted in the following study:

Trends in Social Studies Standards A Scan in the Landscape and Analysis of the Colorado Academic Standards for Social Studies. August 2021 Beth Ratway Edgagement[11]

Fortunately, this study was conducted in time to consider the Fordham Institute Study that ranked Colorado's Social Studies' standards as inadequate with a grade of 'D' in both History and Civics.

Since Colorado's adoption of the most recent standards, a study conducted by the Thomas B. Fordham Institute has been released. In this study, all

50 states' K–12 civics and U.S. history standards were evaluated based on content, rigor, clarity, and organization. Colorado's standards earned a D in both civics and U.S. history, rating the standards as inadequate.[12]

In regard to Native American standards, the Study determined the following:

> Native Americans appear in two standards throughout the document- once in 4th grade and once in 6th grade, in both cases, the standards present Indigenous peoples in past context and do not emphasize native sovereignty nor present day concerns of Indigenous peoples.[13]

In regard to the inclusion of ethnic studies or diverse perspectives, the Study reported:

> Standards only mention race one time throughout the document and this is in preschool. Standards only mention slavery one time and this is in fourth grade.[14]

Clearly the analysis of the CDE's social studies standards from 1998 forward evidence a systemic ethnic cleansing effort in high school education of everything Indian, sanctioned under the color of state law. Colorado simply ignored the legislative mandate of 22-1-104 to require the satisfactory completion of a civil government course for graduation, including the culture, history and social contributions of minorities. I repeat, its illegal diplomas are tainted in the blood, sweat and tears of minority families who want a non-discriminatory education for their children.

2021 CO DOE Standards Review Committee – Social Studies

Five of the thirty-nine members are from the CCSD (12.82%). First draft of the social studies revisions' recommendations will be available for public feedback from November 2021-January 2022. Standards are not expected to be adopted until May-June 2022.[15]

Culturally Responsive Instruction for Native American Students

Title VI, Part A of the Elementary and Secondary Education Act is designed to ensure that American Indian, Native Hawaiian and Alaska Native students meet challenging state academic content and student academic achievement standards, as well as meet their unique culturally related needs.

In 2018, the CDE made the following series available on its Title VI site:

Culturally Responsive Instruction for Native American Students

It currently addresses the following questions:

What is culturally responsive instruction?
Why is it important for Native American students?
How does culturally responsive instruction connect to traditional Native American educational approaches?
What are specific guidelines for providing culturally responsive instruction for Native students?
What does culturally responsive practice look like in different subject areas?
What are the steps to take to develop a culturally responsive practice?[16]

NOTES:

1. https://www.laconiadailysun.com/opinion/letters/common-core-isnt-national-curriculum-or-threaten-state-authority/article_6fe366d6-1a52-527e-9f51-b742155e124a.html (accessed online July 10, 2021).

2. https://web.archive.org/web/20120604213522/http://www.cde.state.co.us/cdeassess/documents/OSA/standards/civics.pdf (accessed online August 15, 2021).

3. https://www.cde.state.co.us/cosocialstudies/cas-socialstudies-p12-pdf (accessed online August 15, 2021).

4. Warner, C.K. (2015). A study of state social studies standards for American Indian education. Multicultural Perspectives, 17(3), 9. *Retrieved from* https://www.researchgate.net/publication/281059261_A_Study_of_State_Social_Studies_Standards_for_American_Indian_Education (accessed online September 5, 2021).

5. https://www.cde.state.co.us/standardsandinstruction/curriculumoverviews-bygrade#HS (accessed online August 15, 2021).

6. https://www.cde.state.co.us/cosocialstudies (accessed online August 15, 2021).

7. https://www.cde.state.co.us/cosocialstudies/statestandards (accessed online August 15, 2021).

8. https://fordhaminstitute.org/sites/default/files/publication/pdfs/20210623-state-state-standards-civics-and-us-history-20210.pdf (accessed online September 5, 2021).

https://www.coloradopolitics.com/opinion/the-podium-colorado-schools-flunk-history/article_ebf7c332-fa6b-11eb-9424-07833425e760.html (accessed online September 5, 2021).

9. https://www.facebook.com/630KHOW/videos/amber-northern-joins-ross/1217136642066940/ June 24, 2021 (accessed online September 5, 2021).

10. https://www.cde.state.co.us/cosocialstudies/benchreport, p.3 (accessed online September 17, 2021).

11. https://www.cde.state.co.us/cosocialstudies/benchreport (accessed online September 17, 2021).

12. Ibid., p. 16.

13. Ibid., pp.19-20.

14. Ibid., p. 19.

15. https://www.cde.state.co.us/standardsandinstruction/group1-socialstudiescommittee
(accessed online September 14, 2021).

16. https://www.cde.state.co.us/cde_english/titlevi (accessed online August 29, 2021).

PART 14 / Holocaust and Genocide Education in Colorado Public Schools

Within less than one year, the CO DOE adopted standards for Holocaust and Genocide Education in Colorado Public Schools. On July 8, 2020, Governor Polis signed into law HB20 – 1336. This legislation includes several elements focusing on the teaching of the Holocaust and Genocide in Colorado. Specifically, on or before July 1, 2023, each school district Board of Education and charter school shall incorporate academic standards on Holocaust and Genocide studies into an existing course that is currently a condition of high school graduation. Said standards shall be recommended by a stakeholder committee and adopted, on or before July 1, 2021, by the State Board of Education and should identify the knowledge and skills that students should acquire related to Holocaust and Genocide studies, including but not limited to the Armenian genocide. In addition, the CDE shall create and maintain a publicly available resource bank of materials pertaining to Holocaust and genocide, no later than July 1, 2021.[1]

NOTES:

1. https://www.cde.state.co.us/cosocialstudies (accessed online August 15, 2021).

PART 15 / CO DOE Graduation Guidelines; CO DOE Consistent in Stating § 22-1-104 Requirement; Yet No Compliance with Graduation Requirement Monitored or Mandated – No Satisfactory Completion of Civil Government Course Required to Graduate, Including History, Culture and Social Contributions of American Indians

CO DOE Purpose of Graduation Guidelines[1]

The CO DOE stated the purpose of its Graduation Guidelines as follows:

> To articulate Colorado's shared belief about the value and meaning of a high school diploma.
> To outline the minimum components, expectations and responsibilities of local districts and the state to support students in attaining a high school diploma.

CO DOE Consistency in Citing Required Compliance with § 22-1-104 Entitled to Judicial Deference

In interpreting §§ 22-1-104 (1)-(6), the CO DOE's authoritative and official position construed the plain language of the statute, considering the explicit language of the statute—"must." This language is not ambiguous. Where the language is plain and its meaning clear, courts will enforce that language as written.

Interpreting §§ 22-1-104 (1)-(6) and incorporating it into the state's graduation requirements is properly within its bailiwick as directed by the Colorado legislature in CRS § 22-2-106.

The CO DOE has consistently maintained the same position in its treatment of § 22-1-104, as it has been revised over time. Its position that compliance with § 22-1-104 is a condition of graduation cannot be countenanced as an 'unfair surprise,' since this has been its historical position.

CO DOE Cites Mandatory Legislative § 22-1-104 Requirement Repeatedly on Its Public Website: Satisfactory Completion of Civil Government Course Required to Graduate, Including History, Culture and Social Contributions of American Indians

> The CO DOE has consistently cited § 22-1-104 as a mandatory state law; its website has numerous specific references, including five as recently as February, July and August 2021.[2]

CO DOE - Graduation Guidelines - March 18, 2021

> Note: *Currently, Colorado's only statewide requirement for high school graduation is the satisfactory completion of a civics/government course that encompasses information on both the United States and State of Colorado (C.R.S. 22-1-104)*
>
> The only course required in state law for graduation is Civics (22-1-104 (3) (a) C.R.S). LEPs have the ability to determine how this course requirement is met.

The CO DOE used the same language in its CDE Graduation Guidelines (GG): Frequently Asked Questions - March 18, 2021, and August 4 and 11, 2021.

CO DOE Monitors School District Compliance with Graduation Guidelines Under an Honor System

The CO DOE monitors school districts compliance with its state Graduation Guidelines under accreditation contracts the school districts file with the CO DOE. The CO DOE is authorized to accredit schools.[3]

> The school districts agree to "substantially comply with all statutory and regulatory requirements applicable to the District…" It is an honor system program as the CO DOE lacks the resources to audit school

district compliance. There are consequences if the CO DOE determines that a school district is violating the state and regulatory requirements. First, the school district would have to be found to have violated the state and regulatory requirements which would require a CO DOE administrative procedure. If a violation is proven to have occurred, the school district will be allowed a time period to come into compliance. If it hasn't based on an administrative review, its accreditation could be impacted.[4]

NOTES:

1. https://slidetodoc.com/colorado-graduation-guidelines-introduction-colorado-is-the-last/ (accessed online July 10, 2021).

2. Colorado Department of Education Cites to 22-1-104 or HB 19-1192
Social Studies, July 1, 2021
www.cde.state.co.us/cosocialstudies (accessed online July 10, 2021).
Graduation Guidelines, August 11, 2021
https://www.cde.state.co.us/postsecondary/graduationguidelines (accessed online August 20, 2021).
Graduation Guidelines Flexibility for the Class of 2021, August 11, 2021
https://www.cde.state.co.us/postsecondary/graduationguidelinesflexibilityaugust2020-2021pdf (accessed online August 20, 2021).
Graduation Guidelines Frequently Asked Questions for Class of 2021, August 4, 2021
https://www.cde.state.co.us/postsecondary/graduationguidelinesfrequentlyaskedquestionsforclassof2021 (accessed online August 20, 2021).
Graduation Guidelines (GG): Frequently Asked Questions
https://www.cde.state.co.us/postsecondary/detailedfaqggreporting (accessed online March 3, 2021).
Reporting Graduation Guidelines PWR Town Hall, February 23, 2021
https://drive.google.com/drive/folders/1KmKcA7wGG_VlTrCFlmxG5MDvSUWHzlsI (accessed online March 23, 2021).
CO DOE Graduation Guidelines Engagement Toolkit
§§ 22-1-104(2) Compliance Required – State Legislated Civics Course
https://www.cde.state.co.us/postsecondary/graduationguidelinesengagementtoolkit (accessed online March 3, 2021).
Graduation Guidelines Flexibility for the Class of 2021
https://www.cde.state.co.us/postsecondary/graduationguidelinesflexibilityaugu

st2020-2021pdf (accessed online March 3, 2021).
Graduation Guidelines Flexibility for the Class of 2021
https://www.cde.state.co.us/postsecondary/graduationguidelinesflexibility2020-2021pdf (accessed online March 3, 2021).
Graduation Guidelines Frequently Asked Questions for Class of 2021
https://www.cde.state.co.us/postsecondary/graduationguidlinesfrequentlyaskedquestionsforclassof2021 (accessed online March 3, 2021).
CO DOE Graduation Guidelines § § 22-1-104
Compliance Required COVID-19 and Graduation 2021
www.cde.state.co.us/postsecondary/graduationguidelines (accessed online March 3, 2021).
Guidelines § § 22-1-104
Compliance Required COVID-19
https://www.cde.state.co.us/postsecondary/graduationguidlinesfaqs (accessed online March 3, 2021).
Contact Person for Graduation Questions: https://www.cde.state.co.us/cdegen/keycontactsatcde (accessed online March 3, 2021).

3. CO DOE District Accountability Handbook, September 2020; https://www.cde.state.co.us/accountability/district-accountability-handbook-2020_final_9-10-2020 (accessed online July 10, 2021).

4. Colorado State Board of Education School District Accreditation Contract
https://www.cde.state.co.us/uip/lisa-medlers-email-communications-with-sample-contract-june-2021 (accessed online July 10, 2021).

CCSD's BOE References Civil Government Graduation Requirement Under § 22-1-104 in Its Graduation Requirements Policy, Yet No Satisfactory Completion of Civil Government Course, Including History, Culture and Social Contributions of American Indians, Actually Required to Graduate

CCSD's BOE References to § 22-1-104 Date Back to 1996, Include Civil Government Graduation Requirement

The CCSD BOE in its 2016, 2018, 2020 Graduation Requirements Policy references § 22-1-104 and "the civics graduation requirement." The CCSD's General Counsel, Ms. Sonja McKenzie, was designated as an Administrator of the Graduation Requirements Policy in 2018 and 2020. Under the Colorado Rules of Professional Conduct applicable to attorneys and as inhouse counsel, she is obligated to inform her client of applicable laws. The CCSD BOE's references to § 22-1-104 also occurred in 1996, 2005 and 2009.

The CCSD's BOE references to § 22-1-104 go back to its Policy on Instructional Resources and Materials, dated August 8, 1966.[1]

> Book: Board Policies
> Section: I. Instruction
> Title: Instructional Resources and Materials
> Code: IJ
> Status: Active
> Adopted: August 8, 1966
> Last Revised: October 9, 2006
>
> As the governing body of the school district, the Board is legally responsible for the selection of all instructional materials.
> Legal
> ...

C.R.S. § 22-1-104(2) (Teaching of History, Culture, and Civil Government)

    Book: Board Policies[2]
    Section: I. Instruction
    Title Basic: Instructional Program
    Code: IHA
    Status: Active
    Adopted: November 14, 2005
    Last Revised: November 9, 2009

The educational program shall provide both formal studies to meet the general academic needs of all students and, to the extent possible, opportunities for individual students to develop specific talents and interest in more specialized fields.

High School Program

    The high school has been designed to serve the needs of students in grades nine through twelve.

    Legal C.R.S. § 22-1-104 (civil government graduation requirement)

Consent Agenda, dated June 13, 2016; Resolution #206-1 June 11, 2018; Resolution #20.11.6 - Approval of Revised Policy IKF, Graduation, November 2020; § 22-1-104(3)(a) (civil government graduation requirement)[3]

    Section I. Instruction
    Title Graduation Requirements
    Code IKF
    Status Active
    Adopted April 10, 2006
    Last Revised November 9, 2020
    Prior Revised Dates
    June 11, 2018, June 13, 2016
    Legal

C.R.S. § 22-1-104(3)(a) (civil government graduation requirement) (**Emphasis added.**)

As of September 11, 2021, the CCSD's BOE website contained no references to any CCSD BOE discussion, meeting or directive regarding § 22-1-104, since November 9, 2020. According to the CCSD, the CCSD BOE has been briefed regarding indigenous parent concerns with § 22-1-104.

CCSD's Administration Has Confirmed Obligatory Status of § 22-1-104

The CCSD administration has also confirmed the obligatory status of § 22-1-104 in (1) an email from Assistant Superintendent Michael Giles to the Indian Parent dated December 5, 2020; and (2) a meeting by Superintendent Siegfried with the IPAC on February 10, 2021.

CCSD's Social Studies Curriculum Does Not Include Civil Government Course, Including History, Culture and Social Contributions of American Indians

However, the CCSD's website fails to demonstrate that its curriculum is in compliance with the present or past § 22-1-104. In fact, the last time the CCSD's social studies curriculum website was updated was on December 4, 2018, prior to HB 19-1192 being signed into law. While the general social studies website was updated on August 19, 2020, there is no reference to § 22-1-104 or any of its requirements.[4]

The CCSD alleges it is in compliance with § 22-1-104, even though it does not yet have a course, because it is waiting for the CO DOE to provide "guidance." On April 12, 2021, the CO DOE did add a webpage including Equity Resources for Districts and BOCES to help "educators bring an equity lens to their systems, policies, and everyday work."[5]

Also, the CCSD initially argued it had six years to conduct a community forum under § 22-1-104. It has since changed its position to one that recognizes the CCSD has had ongoing community forums on this topic, such that it does not need to further satisfy this requirement.

NOTES:

1. https://go.boarddocs.com/co/chcr/Board.nsf/Public# (accessed online March 3, 2021).

2. https://go.boarddocs.com/co/chcr/Board.nsf/Public# (accessed online March 3, 2021).

3. CCSD BOE: 2016 CONSENT AGENDA #08316 JUNE 13, 2016
https://go.boarddocs.com/co/chcr/Board.nsf/Public (accessed online March 3, 2021).
CCSD BOE: 2018 RES. 206-18, June 11, 2018
https://go.boarddocs.com/co/chcr/Board.nsf/Public (accessed online March 3, 2021).
CCSD BOE: 2020 RES. 20.11.6, Nov. 9, 2020
https://go.boarddocs.com/co/chcr/Board.nsf/Public (accessed online March 3, 2021).

4. https://www.cherrycreekschools.org/Page/2946. https://www.cherrycreekschools.org/domain/2320 (accessed online March 3, 2021).

5. https://www.cde.state.co.us/equityresourcesfordistrictsandboces (accessed online May 18, 2021).

PART 17 / CCSD's Curriculum Review with Racial and Cultural Relevance Focus for Kindergarten through Fifth Grade.

CCSD's Superintendent Email Message to Parents on April 23, 2021, regarding Curriculum Review with Racial and Cultural Relevance Focus for Kindergarten through Fifth Grade

On April 23, 2021, the CCSD's Superintendent Dr. Scott Siegfried advised parents in an email message that the CCSD intended to implement a curriculum review to **revise current social studies standards for kindergarten through fifth grade**:

> As part of our Future Forward strategic plan, we are working collaboratively with teachers and administrators to review existing curricular resources through a lens of racial and cultural relevance…It is critical that we identify resources that accurately reflect the contributions and narratives of our diverse community.

This email message is not available online so the limited information provided is from the article in The Villager newspaper.[1]

CCSD's Parents' Respond to Superintendent Siegfried's Email Message to Parents on CCSD Curriculum Review with Racial and Cultural Relevance Focus for Kindergarten through Fifth Grade

At the end of the regular meeting of the CCSD BOE on May 10, 2021, several parents from a full house of spectators at the in-person and virtual meeting rose to address the CCSD BOE about Superintendent Siegfried's message. One parent adverse to the planned revision in curriculum stated:

> It is a shock… to realize the importance and potential impact of this

decision...that the curriculum should include the ideas and mythology of critical race theory. While on the surface, this perspective seems positive, the result is the opposite of healing and will ultimately bring further division.

Another parent argued that:

> Our schools are teaching that America...is a nation of systemic oppression and inequalities, causing students to feel ashamed and resentful of being American. ... I've noticed an urgency to reform and morph curriculum surrounding recent social and political movements...regarding critical race theory...and the Colorado bill HB19-1192...

As noted by the reporter covering this event, "critical race theory" is not mentioned anywhere in the statute or in Superintendent Siegfried's message to parents.[2]

Critical Race Theory

According to *Education Week*,

> Critical Race Theory is an academic concept that's causing a stir in education systems nationwide. Critical Race Theory is an academic concept with the core idea that racism is a social construct that's embedded in social, legal and political systems.[3]
>
> Supporters of critical race theory say that its teachings show how race is implemented into history and becomes systemic in a community's or country's institutions—business, legal, health, criminal justice, etc. Critics say the theory is divisive and discriminatory.

It has become a lightning rod across the country to challenge the inclusion of the history of minorities in public schools. Twenty-five states have taken steps to prohibit or limit the teaching of critical race theory or to restrict how teachers can discuss racism and sexism, according to a recent analysis by Education Week. It is uncertain whether this legislation is constitutional. Most likely, it will be attacked for at a minimum, vagueness.

CCSD's Media Response to Parents' Concerns at CCSD BOE Meeting regarding Curriculum Review with Racial and Cultural Relevance Focus for Kindergarten through Fifth Grade

A local newspaper, *The Villager*, reached out to the CCSD for a response to these concerns. On May 19, 2021, the CCSD stated:

> We are already in the process of reviewing curriculum and instructional materials to ensure they are aligned to our values of inclusivity and racial and cultural equity. Teachers are getting ongoing training and support about state standards and how to apply them through a culturally responsive lens.[4]

NOTES:

1. CCSD Parents Question Potential Social Studies Curriculum Changes, The Villager, May 26, 2021, Freda Miklin
https://villagerpublishing.com/ccsd-parents-question-potential-social-studies-curriculum-changes (accessed online July 10, 2021).

2. CCSD Parents Speak Out on Issues of Race and Inclusivity in Curriculum, The Villager, May 19, 2021, Freda Miklin
https://villagerpublishing.com/ccsd-parents-speak-out-on-issues-of-race-and-inclusivity-in-curriculum/ (accessed online July 10, 2021).

3. https://www.edweek.org/leadership/what-is-critical-race-theory-and-why-is-it-under-attack/2021/05 (accessed online July 10, 2021).

4. CCSD Parents Speak Out on Issues of Race and Inclusivity in Curriculum, The Villager, May 19, 2021, Freda Miklin
https://villagerpublishing.com/ccsd-parents-speak-out-on-issues-of-race-and-inclusivity-in-curriculum/ (accessed online June 1, 2021).

PART 18 / CCSD's Social Studies Curricular Resource Review Implementation Scheduled for 2024-2025 - No Mention Whatsoever of § 22-1-104

CCSD's Social Studies Curricular Resource Review Implementation Scheduled for 2024-2025 - No Mention Whatsoever of § 22-1-104

On April 23, 2021, the CCSD's Social Studies Curricular Resource Review was presented to the CCSD BOE reflecting a timeline of possible implementation of Social Studies curriculum revisions in 2024-2025. There is no mention whatsoever of § 22-1-104. The schedule presented to the CCSD BOE states:

> Transition: Plan and Design will be developed in 2022-2023.
>
> Transition: Test and Refine will be done in 2023-2024.
>
> ***Implementation is not scheduled until 2024-2025.***
>
> Implementation and Refine is scheduled for 2025-2026
>
> Subsequent Revision 2026-2027. (Emphasis added.)

The CCSD's Curricular Resource Review to Align with Colorado Academic Standards process includes:

> Review CDE content standard changes and/or updates and provide our educators with professional learning at the building and classroom level on how these standards have changed.
>
> Bring collaborative stakeholder groups together to identify curricular resources to align with the Colorado Academic Standards.

Create a professional development plan for the rollout of the new or updated curricular resources.

Sarah Grobbel, CCSD's Assistant Superintendent for Career, Innovation, and Student Engagement reported that the HB 19-1192 Commission began meeting in 2019 and gave its completed recommendations to CDE just last month. "Next," she said, "CDE will spend this whole next year ... looking at what the new revised standards should be based on those recommendations, while the commission spends the next two years curating different curricular resources that they can share across Colorado to our school districts." Then CCSD "will have two years after we get the new revised standards to transition, plan, design, then test and refine the instruction that we are going to put in front of our kids before we fully implement (the revised standards)" in the 2024-2025 school year, according to the illustrative timeline presented at the meeting.[1]

The CCSD does not believe it has to comply with § 22-1-104 until the CO DOE issues "guidance" specific to § 22-1-104. Also, there is concern with introducing these topics if teachers do not have a "culturally responsive lens." More harm may be done than good. There is no schedule for when teachers may be significantly ready to teach with the appropriate 'lens.' Colorado Open Records requests by the Indian Parent on November 19, 2020, and subsequently on April 2, 2021, did not provide any information regarding a § 22-1-104 curriculum.

CCSD's plan is not in accord with the statute.

Number 1: As of 2007, they should have already been teaching a civil government course with Indian history, culture and social contributions, and **no** student should have been allowed to graduate without successfully completing this course. ....

Number 2. No statute permits "CDE this whole next year...looking at what the new revised standards should be based on those recommendations, while the commission spends the next two years curating different curricular resources that they can share across Colorado to our school districts."[2]

Number 3. No statute permits CCSD another two years after that to implement § 22-2-104(1).

June 23, 2021, CCSD BOE Meeting: CCSD's Curriculum Review Process

The CCSD presented in part, briefly, at the June 23, 2021, CO BOE meeting, a PowerPoint regarding the planned Social Studies Curricular Resource Review. It did not refer to § 22-1-104 or any state or local laws or regulations applicable to the time periods required for the CO DOE or the CCSD to implement new curriculum. CCSD's Social Studies Curricular Resource Review is the sole creation of the CCSD.

In an article in The Villager newspaper by Freda Miklin, Government Reporter Miklin explained CCSD's process of curriculum review as presented by the CCSD at the June 23, 2021, meeting.

Sarah Grobbel, CCSD's Assistant Superintendent for Career, Innovation, and Student Engagement, and Dr. Dominique Jones, CCSD's Director of Curriculum and Instruction, explained the process that leads to changes in curriculum at the CCSD:

> It begins with the Colorado Department of Education (CDE) which develops the statewide Colorado Academic Standards (CAS), subject to regular revision. When school districts like Cherry Creek receive revisions to the CAS, Grobbel explained, "We take those revisions, we start to dig into them, we talk about what they mean inside of instruction in classrooms and lesson planning. We align different curricular resources in order to teach those to the best of our ability. Then we provide ongoing professional learning and our teachers also collaborate in professional learning communities in order to focus on the best instructional practices… to meet…the excellence you expect…in the classroom."

> Sarah Grobbel continued:

> When new legislation is passed by the state legislature that impacts CAS, such as occurred two years ago with HB19-1192, Inclusion of American Minorities in Teaching Civil Government, "it doesn't jump directly to the schools," Grobbel said, "it goes through a process where CDE has to look at the legislation…and in this case, go from the commission and (its) recommendations to CDE. Then they go through an adoption period where they revise the CAS, which continue to be our guideline for all the work that we do in all of our classrooms."

> Grobbel reported that the HB 19-1192 Commission began meeting in 2019

and gave its completed recommendations to CDE just last month. "Next," she said, "CDE will spend this whole next year...looking at what the new revised standards should be based on those recommendations, while the commission spends the next two years curating different curricular resources that they can share across Colorado to our school districts." Then CCSD "will have two years after we get the new revised standards to transition, plan, design, then test and refine the instruction that we are going to put in front of our kids before we fully implement (the revised standards)" in the 2024-2025 school year, according to the illustrative timeline presented at the meeting.

In order to respond to the needs of CCSD students, parents, and the community, as well as the goals of the new law, Dr. Jones described a project-based learning model that was used to help **revise current social studies standards for kindergarten through fifth grade**. It is aligned to state standards, student centered, identifies connections to students' interactions with their community, and contains diverse representation of American minorities' contributions, consistent with the goals of HB19-1192. Before it was approved, a group of 21 stakeholder parents, teachers, coaches and school administrators representing diverse geographical areas, races, genders, and roles in their organization, reviewed it in great depth over several days using objective criteria.[3]

August 9, 2021, CCSD BOE Meeting

Further discussion occurred at the August 9, 2021, CCSD BOE Meeting on the § 22-1-104 statute and the need for a more inclusive curriculum by parents and students.

Carol Harvey, a resident of the CCSD, advised the CCSD BOE that if it wasn't complying with § 22-1-104, it must **report its non-compliance** to the CDE or be in breach of its contract filed with the CDE, assuring Cherry Creek's compliance with all applicable statutory requirements.[4] Her statement below was provided to the CCSD BOE and media.

> Good evening. Forty-eight years ago, the Colorado legislature mandated public school instruction about Spanish Americans and Negroes (C.R.S. 1973, 123-21-4). Twenty-five years ago American Indians were added. Eighteen years ago, the legislature added the satisfactory completion of a civil government course as a condition of high school

graduation, which included instruction about the history, culture and contributions of African and Hispanic Americans and American Indians, starting in Two Thousand Seven (SB 36 - C.R.S. 2003, § 21-1-104). In Two Thousand Nineteen, Asian-Americans, LGBTQ individuals and religious minorities were added, with immediate effect (HB 19-1192).

Required compliance with this statute, § 22-1-104, is repeatedly stated on the Colorado Department of Education's website.

The Colorado Attorney General in 1983 and the judiciary in 1994 upheld § 22-1-104. A Two Thousand Three federal case, cited § 22-1-104, in dicta, as an example of a valid curriculum requirement. Cherry Creek was a defendant in that case. Cherry Creek's Graduation Requirements, promulgated unanimously by its Board in Two Thousand Sixteen, Two Thousand Eighteen and Two Thousand Twenty, cite § 22-1-104(3)(a) and its [quote] "civil government graduation requirement." [close quote]

If Cherry Creek isn't requiring the satisfactory completion of a § 22-1-104 course as a condition of high school graduation, it must report its non-compliance to the Colorado Department of Education (CDE) or be in breach of its contract filed with the CDE, assuring Cherry Creek's compliance with all applicable statutory requirements. It can't wait four more years or longer to comply.

Significantly, the CDE's Two Thousand Eighteen Report to the U.S. Department of Education on federal funding for Individuals with Disabilities specifically cites § 22-1-104's course and graduation requirements.

As statewide compliance with § 22-1-104 is questionable, Governor Polis must determine if there is a countenanced, systemic violation of § 22-1-104 ongoing which could impact (1) public schools' accreditation; (2) federal funding; (3) the legally protected classes under § 22-1-104; (4) the constitutionally protected property interest of students to a valid diploma; and (5) public safety, given the militia's engagement. Thank you.

Individuals with Disabilities Education Act Colorado Department of Education Performance Plan PART B, P. 7 , www.cde.state.co.us/cdesped/spp-apr

Provide a narrative that describes the conditions youth must meet in order to graduate with a regular high school diploma and, if different, the conditions that youth with IEPs must meet in order to graduate with a regular high school diploma. If there is a difference, explain.

Under Colorado law, "each school district board of education retains the authority to develop its own unique high school graduation requirements, so long as those local high school graduation requirements meet or exceed any minimum standards or basic core competencies or skills identified in the comprehensive set of guidelines for high school graduation developed by the state board pursuant to this paragraph." 22-2-106(1)(a.5) C.R.S. There are no specific courses, or numbers of courses, required by the state's graduation guidelines, and there are no legislated course requirements other than one course in Civics: "Satisfactory completion of a course on the civil government of the United States and the state of Colorado . . . shall be a condition of high school graduation in the public schools of this state." 22-1-104 (3)(a) C.R.S. Youth with IEPs must meet the same requirements as youth without IEPs in order to graduate with a regular high school diploma.

ATTORNEY GENERAL AND STATE AND FEDERAL CASE CITES

1983 CO Attorney General Opinion 983 Colo. AG LEXIS 33 (Dec. 2, 1983)

Skipworth v. Board of Educ., 874 P. Ed. 487 (1994)

Lane v. Owens, U.S. District Court of Colorado, Civil Docket Case No 1:03-cv-01544-LTB, Judge Lewis T. Babcock, August 15, 2003, Ruling (pp. 6-7)

JEFFCO Social Studies Curriculum Update

https://www.thepulsefromcandi.com/blog/category/socialstudies

To comply with CDE's Two Thousand Twenty (2020) Civics Standards and House Bill 19-1192, Jefferson County's School District updated its Civics Units of Study in February Two Thousand Twenty (2020).

INTERNET CITES of § 22-1-104

"Colorado in particular has one of the most robust civics education requirements in the country. In fact, the only statewide graduation requirement in Colorado is the completion of a civics and government course. Colorado designed curriculum for a full year civics course, and provides a myriad of resources and guidance for teachers on the subject."
https://populationeducation.org/an-essential-guide-to-civics-education-in-the-united-states-today/

Education Commission of the States Colorado: Public schools are required to teach a course on the history and civil government of the state of Colorado and the United States, to include the history, culture and contributions of minorities. Satisfactory completion of this course is required for high school graduation. C.R.S. 22-1-104

https://www.csmonitor.com/Media/Content/2018/0323/0323-civics-map
https://www.edweek.org/teaching-learning/data-most-states-require-history-but-not-civics
https://ecs.secure.force.com/mbdata/MBQuest2RTANW?Rep=CIP1601S
https://www.americanprogress.org/issues/education-k-12/reports/2018/02/21/446857/state-civics-education/
https://www.aft.org/ae/summer2018/shapiro_brown
https://medium.com/generation-citizen/mapping-the-civic-education-policy-landscape-9e5766692efe

The handout also included the CCSD BOE 2016, 2018 and 2020 Graduation Requirements Policies.

Julie Jaeger, CCSD's Executive Director, High School Education, and other administrative officials, contend CCSD is in compliance with § 22-1-104.

NOTES:

1. Regular Board of Education Meeting, April 23, 2021, Board of Education, Cherry Creek School District
https://go.boarddocs.com/co/chcr/Board.nsf/Public (accessed online July 10, 2021).

2. Creek Schools: We Don't Teach Critical Race Theory, The Villager, June 30, 2021, Freda Miklin
https://villagerpublishing.com/cherry-creek-schools-we-dont-teach-critical-race-theory/ (accessed online July 10, 2021).

3. Regular Board of Education Meeting, June 23, 2021, Board of Education, Cherry Creek School District
https://go.boarddocs.com/co/chcr/Board.nsf/Public (accessed online July 10, 2021).

4. Colorado State Board of Education School District Accreditation Contract
https://www.cde.state.co.us/uip/lisa-medlers-email-communications-with-sample-contract-june-2021 (accessed online July 10, 2021).
CO DOE District Accountability Handbook, September 2020; https://www.cde.state.co.us/accountability/district-accountability-handbook-2020_final_9-10-2020 (accessed online July 10, 2021).

PART 19 / CCSD BOE Meeting, September 13, 2021, Minority Academic Achievement Gap, Discipline Statistics for Minorities Continue to Demonstrate Pattern of Disparate Impact - Include American Indians

CCSD BOE/ District Leadership Team Study Session, Sep. 10, 2021 – Focus on Minority Academic Achievement Gap

The Equity, Culture and Community Engagement Agenda topic was removed from the Agenda.

Colorado Measures of Academic Success ("CMAS") Testing

The CMAS testing results were on the Agenda. They reflected the continuing Academic Achievement Gap from 2017 between CCSD White students and Students of Color. Board Member Angela Garland questioned if the CMAS testing is a test of affluence, rather than ability. With the wealth factor of families in the CCSD, many students have the opportunity to take advance PSAT and advance SAT testing so they are better prepared for the tests. They have family opportunities for encouraging scholastic, homework and extra-curricular activities. Students of poverty simply do not have the same access, home environment and many of them work and are precluded from after-school activities. She is concerned with the ongoing Academic Achievement Gap from 2017 between CCSD White students and Students of Color. She is also concerned with the impact racism may play. Board member Janice McDonald voiced her concern regarding the Academic Achievement Gap from 2017 between CCSD White students and Students of Color.

CCSD BOE Study Session, 5 PM, September 13, 2021 – Focus on Safety Due to Past Presence of Militia and Unruly Public

The Board discussed their fear of the possibility of violence at the 7 PM CCSD BOE meeting. They were concerned they could be targeted by the militia and their family and homes threatened. They were also concerned that they and the public were being "terrorized" by a "hostile, violent, aggressive" public element "trying to intimidate" them and those in attendance. This group is opposed to curriculum change and "diversity." Residents of the District were afraid to attend, which would eliminate their opportunity for being heard. Thirty-six speakers had signed up.

The security program for the meeting was presented and a secure location for the Board had been set up in the event of a disruption of the meeting.

Karen Fisher, Chair of CCSD BOE, confirmed that the minority children speakers would be present and speak at the meeting.

CCSD BOE Meeting, September 13, 2021 – Focus on Minority Academic Achievement Gap, Discipline Statistics for Minorities Continue to Demonstrate Pattern of Disparate Impact

The meeting was **heavily guarded by armed security**, with one person escorted out, before the meeting started, by the police. Flashing red police vehicle lights in the parking lot were visible in the darkness outside throughout the meeting. At one point, a group of about six fully attired firemen walked through the meeting area.

For some reason, the CCSD had a number of minority children from elementary to high school speak about their school experience. I did not listen as I considered it horribly offensive and abusive to put these children in danger and parade them out to speak on behalf of the CCSD. After they spoke, they were escorted out by armed guards. It reminded me of the argument that even if slavery is cruel and degrading, the slaves were happy. It appeared to be an effort to discredit the CCSD's minority communities' concerns.

E. W. Clays print of a slave owning family conveys this same idea:

> "...an attractive and wealthy, slave-owning white family, including a husband, his wife, and their two children. The young daughter plays with a lean greyhound which stands before them. The son gestures toward an elderly black couple with a small child sitting at their feet. A group of happy slaves dance in the background. The old slave says, "God Bless you

massa! you feed and clothe us. When we are sick you nurse us, and when too old to work, you provide for us!" The master vows piously, "These poor creatures are a sacred legacy from my ancestors and while a dollar is left me, nothing shall be spared to increase their comfort and happiness." [1]

A Special Report on Equity, Culture and Community Engagement was given to the Board by Assistant Superintendent Michael Giles and his staff from the Office of Inclusive Excellence ("OIE"). The website states the "OIE serves as a critical liaison between the district and its diverse community, working to promote racial, ethnic, linguistic, religious, sexual orientation, gender identity, and cultural understandings which form productive partnerships resulting in an inclusive learning community for all!"[2]

While focused on the path forward they are trying to create, Mr. Giles stated in his PowerPoint presentation that the minority Academic Achievement Gap has been "consistent, pervasive and predictable."[3] By "predictable," he meant a statistical trend analysis would justify such a conclusion.

Also, he stated the discipline statistics for minorities continue to demonstrate a pattern of disparate impact.[4] A Discipline Chart is shown on p. 18 of the Equity, Culture and Community Engagement presentation with little change in discipline disparities from 2015-2020[5] His presentation did not address minority curriculum or § 22-1-104.

Board Member Angela Garland asked Assistant Superintendent Giles **when** they would close the continuing Academic Achievement Gap. In a strong statement, she said the glossy photographs of smiling minority children did not do justice to the underlying problems of minority student achievement and disciplinary disparities.

CCSD BOE Meeting, September 13, 2021, Carol Harvey's Public Comment

The reason I got involved in fighting for a more inclusive curriculum is because of the struggle the Indigenous parents in the CCSD have had for the past decade petitioning for an Indian curriculum. At the CCSD IPAC Meeting on November 18, 2020, Rep. Gonzales-Gutierrez, a legislative sponsor of HB 19-1192, codified as § 22-1-104(1), stated that there was no enforcement component to it; it had "no teeth." The meeting generated significant emotional distress, to the point of sobbing, among its Indigenous parent participants. I could not stand idly by in the face of this injustice.

I consider the countenanced, systemic, willful defiance of the legislatively mandated § 22-1-104 statute a genocidal, ethnic cleansing effort of everything Indian, sanctioned under the color of state law. CCSD's illegal diplomas are tainted in the blood, sweat and tears of minority families who want an education for their children in which they see themselves.

The U.S. Civil Rights Commission stated in 2018 that a lack of American Indian Curriculum Can (1) Be Harmful to American Indian Students; (2) Contribute to a Negative Learning Environment; (3) Be Isolating and Limiting; (4) Trigger Bullying; and (5) Result in Negative Stereotypes Across the Board. This is true for all minority students.

In 1877, Commissioner of Indian Affairs Hayt reported to the Secretary of the Interior that all Indians in Colorado should be removed to the Indian Territory, in what is now Oklahoma. Miners, in search of gold and silver, could claim lands without regard to Indian reservations. All of the arable land was required by white settlers and feeding them was of paramount importance.

In not teaching a civil government course which includes Indian history, culture and social contributions, you are effectively removing Indian students from your District. The prize of education becomes paramount only for white children.

A school superintendent in Arizona described his strategy against Mexican American studies by doing what "Hannibal did to the Romans, and when Hannibal encountered the Romans he stretched them out" ... during which time the school district lost an enormous number of their Mexican–American students.

I hope CCSD will not use this tactic. Thank you.

Media Coverage of September 13, 2021, Meeting, Especially CCSD's Attempts to Close Academic Achievement Gap for Students of Color

As reported in *The Sentinel Newspaper*,

The district has had various equity programs and committees beginning in the 1980s, and this is the latest configuration in a long series of efforts to boost the performance of students of color and prepare them for a career.

The department seeks to close achievement gaps in a number of ways. Those include increasing hiring and retention of teachers of color, creating more opportunities for parents from diverse backgrounds to connect with the district and advocate for their children, creating more college and career readiness programs and partnering with outside organizations to support students.

Angela Garland and Janice McDonald, the board's two Black members, both voiced frustration at the meeting that the district is still struggling to meet the needs of students of color.
"It is troubling to hear the same things over and over and over again and not see them change," McDonald said. "But I do hope we will begin to see the needle move."

"It's disappointing that we're one of the top districts in the country and we still can't get this right," board member Angela Garland said.
Garland spoke about some of the difficulties her own son has encountered in school, such as teachers not knowing how to handle racial slurs in books being read in class.

She also said she was hurt by allegations that wanting to ensure that students have a diverse curriculum is divisive or unpatriotic. "Our kids learn about the Holocaust," she said. "We've never gotten emailed about that, nor should we. These comments about being un-American, being oppressive, that's ridiculous. That's our story, that's everyone's story."[6]

CCSD BOE Limits Public Comment to People with Connections to District

The CCSD BOE revised its public comment policy on September 13, 2021, to clarify that speakers must reside within the district or have some connection to Cherry Creek.

District spokesperson Abbe Smith said that there have been numerous instances over the past several months of people coming to speak at the board meetings who do not live in the area and are not connected to the district. Several of the board's past meetings have been dominated by hours of contentious public comment about mask mandates and critical race theory.[7]

NOTES:

1. https://www.loc.gov/pictures/resource/cph.3g05950/ (accessed online September 14, 2021).

2. https://www.cherrycreekschools.org/Page/2846 (accessed online September 14, 2021).

3. Cherry Creek Department of Equity, Culture, and Community Engagement Presentation, p. 19 https://go.boarddocs.com/co/chcr/Board.nsf/files/C6VTCZ755047/$file/BOE%20Presentation%20Sept%2013%202021.pdf / (accessed online September 14, 2021)

4. Audio recording of CCSD BOE Meeting, Sep. 13, 2021, 55 Minute Mark. https://cherrycreekschoolsorg-my.sharepoint.com/:u:/g/personal/jkoenig6_cherrycreekschools_org/ERRI1UyB3FFAoBHSmhjgd5ABzoWCPy4-GwrE_Ur3Xfp5AQ?e=3Rwq7b (accessed online September 15, 2021).

5. CCSD Discipline Chart Cherry Creek Department of Equity, Culture, and Community Engagement Presentation, p. 18. https://go.boarddocs.com/co/chcr/Board.nsf/files/C6VTCZ755047/$file/BOE%20Presentation%20Sept%2013%202021.pdf / (accessed online September 14, 2021).

6. https://sentinelcolorado.com/orecent-headlines/cherry-creek-school-district-moving-ahead-with-more-equity-programs-to-close-achievement-gaps/ (accessed online September 14, 2021).

7. https://sentinelcolorado.com/orecent-headlines/new-cherry-creek-school-district-policy-limits-public-comment-to-people-with-connections-to-district/ (accessed online September 16, 2021).

PART 20 / CCSD's Office of Inclusive Excellence ("OIE") Partnerships for Academically Successful Students (P.A.S.S.) Indigenous Parent Action Committee ("IPAC") Meetings -Indigenous Parents Had Petitioned CCSD for American Indian Curriculum for Over a Decade

CCSD's Office of Inclusive Excellence ("OIE") Partnerships for Academically Successful Students (P.A.S.S.) September 16, 2020 Goals

OIE, in writing, stated one of its goals is to focus on the CCSD's curriculum— "To offer a more complete, accurate lens of the content in the curriculum – HB 19-1192 ..."[1]

P.A.S.S. IPAC Meetings

The OIE has hosted several meetings with the IPAC discussing the need for a more inclusive curriculum. See Minutes.[2]

October 27, 2020, IPAC Public Meeting

The possibility of litigation against the CCSD regarding compliance with § 22-1-104 is documented in the October 27, 2020, IPAC Minutes.

November 18, 2020, IPAC Public Meeting - No Enforcement Component to § 22-1-104; It Had "No Teeth"

At the CCSD IPAC Public Meeting on November 18, 2020, Rep. Gonzales-Gutierrez, a legislative sponsor of HB 19-1192, spoke on §§ 22-1-104 (1)-(6) (aka HB 19-1192). Rep. Gonzales-Gutierrez stated that there was no enforcement component to §§ 22-1-104 (1)-(6); it had "no teeth." The meeting generated significant emotional distress, to the point of sobbing, among its indigenous parent participants. There was concern of a divide and conquer approach being imposed by the CCSD creating a chilling effect on participation. There was also concern that the uncertainty of when the CCSD would comply would emotionally wear down the indigenous parents who have sought inclusion of indigenous curriculum for a decade. The CCSD indigenous parents' concern is not unfounded.

In litigation, a school superintendent in Arizona described his strategy against Mexican American studies by doing what "Hannibal did to the Romans, and when Hannibal encountered the Romans he stretched them out ... during which time the school district "lost an enormous number of their Mexican–American Stud[ies] students." Jaramillo, Nathalia E. Arizona, Hannibal's Cowboys, and the Modern Day Tie-Down, Pages 119-124, Published online: Dec. 11, 2012. (Accessed May 18, 2021). The case was filed on October 1, 2010, with a final decision on August 21, 2017.

In response to the HB 19-1192 CCSD presentation, the concerned Indian Parent submitted the following written questions in writing, pursuant to CCSD protocol:

> Is the CCSD currently teaching a civil government class to comply with HB 19-1192?
>
> If the CCSD is found to have violated a state law, such as not teaching a mandatory civil government class to comply with HB 19-1192, does that jeopardize its state accreditation?
>
> Is there any possible impact on federal or state funding based on non-compliance with a state law?
>
> As all parents and guardians have the legal right to be informed regarding compliance with HB 19-1192, will the CCSD inform parents and guardians what has been done or is being done to ensure compliance with the Act?
>
> Has the CCSD established any policies relative to compliance with HB 19-1192?

November 19, 2020, IPAC Member Letter to Superintendent re Compliance with § 22-1-104; Letter re Community Forum

The Indian Parent also submitted two letters concerning the CCSD's compliance with §§ 22-1-104(1) and (2), addressed to the CCSD Superintendent's Seigfried.

The letters were hand-delivered to the CCSD, copies of which were stamped by CCSD personnel evidencing receipt by the CCSD. No response has been received to his letters. In fact, the CCSD denies having received these letters.

November 19, 2020, IPAC Member CORA Request to CCSD

On November 19, 2020, the Indian Parent submitted a Colorado Open Records Request to the CCSD for any and all CCSD records from February 1, 2019 through November 19, 2020, related to (1) House Bill 19-1192; and/or (2) information pertaining to ethnic studies or related curriculum; and/or (3) graduation requirements pertaining to House Bill 19-1192.

The request included CCSD records relating to:

> "Emails notifying members of the community or students of any discussions on HOUSE BILL 19-1192;
>
> Determining policies relative to (1) HOUSE BILL 19-1192; and/or (2) ethnic studies or related curriculum;
>
> Developing strategy relative to (1) HOUSE BILL 19-1192; and/or (2) ethnic studies or related curriculum;
>
> Risk analyses pertaining to compliance or non-compliance with (1) HOUSE BILL 19-1192; (2) ethnic studies or related curriculum requirements; and/or (3) any effect on graduation requirements;
>
> Notices to students, parents or guardians of the requirements of (1) HOUSE BILL 19-1192 and how the CCSD intends to comply with it;
>
> Any records regarding the allocation or expenditure of public funds including contracts, bids, requests for proposals, and any other business record involving the expenditure of public funds relative to (1) HOUSE BILL 19-1192; and/or (2) ethnic studies or related curriculum;
>
> Conferences with an attorney or legal representative for purposes of receiving advice on specific legal questions pertaining to HOUSE BILL 19-1192; (2) ethnic studies or related curriculum; and/or (3) graduation requirements; and...
>
> Any other applicable records."

December 5, 2020, CCSD's OIE Willing to Discuss § 22-1-104 with IPAC Member

The Assistant Superintendent overseeing the OIE offered to discuss § 22-1-104 with the Indian Parent. The Indian Parent was concerned about any confusion or misunderstanding that might result from a private meeting. He elected to only communicate in writing. Also, he considered it more appropriate, necessary and important for the CCSD to communicate on this issue in public.

December 8, 2020, IPAC Public Meeting

OIE stated that the written questions submitted by the Indian Parent on November 18, 2020, had been referred to the CCSD's Superintendent and the CCSD's General Counsel for response.

December 10, 2020, CCSD's CORA Response to IPAC Member

The only documents provided to the CORA request were the following:

> 08/05/2019: Request for nomination by indigenous parent to serve on the HB 19-1192 Task Force
> 08/17/2020: Colorado Springs Equity Policy Statement
> 09/14/2020: District P.A.S.S. Steering Committee Meeting Minutes
> 10/27/2020: CCSD Indian Education Meeting
> 11/09/2020: Request from CCSD's Office of Inclusive Excellence to State Rep. Gonzales-Gutierrez to speak about House Bill 19-1192 at District P.A.S.S. Meeting
> 11/17/2020: Public Invitation from CCSD's Office of Inclusive Excellence to public virtual District P.A.S.S. meeting on November 18, 2020, at which State Rep. Gonzales-Gutierrez would speak about House Bill 19-1192.

The CCSD also stated as follows:

> "Developing strategy relative to HB 19-1192 and/or ethnic studies or related curriculum. No responsive documents;
>
> Risk analyses pertaining to compliance or non-compliance with HB 19-1192; ethnic studies or related curriculum requirements; and/or any effect on graduation requirements. No responsive documents;

Any records regarding the allocation of public funds including contracts, bids, requests for proposals and any other business record involving the expenditures of public funds relative to HB 19-1192 or ethnic studies and related curriculum. No responsive documents as described;

Conferences with an attorney or legal representative for purposes of receiving advise on specific legal questions pertaining to HB 19-1192, ethnic studies or related curriculum, and/or graduation requirements. Withheld pursuant to attorney/client privilege."

The CCSD failed to include the CCSD's BOE Minutes and Adoption of Graduation Requirements specifically referencing § 22-1-104(3)(a) (civil government graduation requirement), Resolution #20.11.6 - Approval of Revised Policy IKF, Graduation Requirements and Exhibit IKF-E, Options to Demonstrate College and Career Preparedness, dated November 9, 2020.

In addition, the CCSD failed to include the Office of Inclusive Excellence Partnerships for Academically Successful Students (P.A.S.S.) Presentation, dated September 16, 2020, which stated one of the District P.A.S.S. 2020-2021 Goals was: "To offer a more complete, accurate lens of the content in the curriculum – HB 19-1192 ..."

January 12, 2021, IPAC Public Meeting

The IPAC Meeting in January 2021 also contained no feedback to the questions regarding § 22-1-104 submitted to the OIE on November 18, 2020.

February 10, 2021, IPAC Public Meeting

The CCSD's Superintendent Siegfried participated in the February 10, 2021, IPAC Meeting and advised the following: he had the authority to piecemeal a class together from other courses that students had already completed during high school (e.g., History, English, Government) to satisfy the civil government course requirement in § 22-1-104. He had consulted with the CCSD General Counsel, Sonja McKenzie, and was advised that (i) he did not need to establish the legislatively mandated course; (ii) he had the authority to designate a course from past courses that would satisfy the § 22-1-104 course requirement; and (3) high school diplomas could be issued and that there would not be a problem with the legality of such diplomas. Parents did not need to worry.

Curriculum content is NOT a course. In 'fabricating' a content course, the CCSD will have to subtract from existing courses. Uniformity, transferability, class hours, method to measure credit and grade assessment will be impossible. No existing courses in the CCSD's High School Registration Guides describe the content requirements of § 22-1-104. For example, the Grandview High School Registration Guide has 715 references to 'course.' Credit is received for the satisfactory completion of a course. There are no content references to Indian, Asian, gay, lesbian, bisexual, transgender, queer, and one each to Latino(a) [Latin American in Advanced Placement Spanish Literature and culture course] and African American [Concurrent Enrollment Survey of African-American Literature]. These two courses are open to a select few students.[3]

Pursuant to § 22-2-116.5, C.R.S., Colorado requires reporting by school districts of courses satisfactorily completed by students, not content. There is no identified course by number and description of the content. There are no scheduled minutes of instruction offering contact with faculty with students in a given term, utilizing a particular method of instruction. There is no course type such as a lecture or lab. There is no faculty or time or location specified for such a course. There is no procedure to register for such a course.

February 17, 2021, IPAC Public Meeting

On February 17, 2021, the CCSD requested and provided a public virtual forum for the indigenous group to discuss concerns with § 22-1-104. A one-hour public ZOOM presentation, along with a panel discussion, was advertised and hosted by the CCSD, on February 17, 2021. The Indian Parent provided a PowerPoint presentation and Panel discussion with issues of concern.

CCSD parents, as well as other school district individuals, participated. Questions were permitted and answers provided. CCSD's administrative personnel attended and had every opportunity to further the discussion around the missing § 22-1-104 course which they failed to do. No response to this presentation has been received from the CCSD or the CCSD's BOE.

Let Indigenous Voices Be Heard

https://www.cherrycreekschools.org/Page/4013

https://cherrycreekschools-org.zoom.us/meeting/register/tJYsdOurpjoiE9en9xS8GQC27APEVClN4zU_

Link: https://teamup.com/event/show/id/
qFwkQWEi5vjFwDPXoA7s7B9sAef6oq

August 26, 2021, IPAC Meeting, ESSER Funds

The CCSD received from the Elementary and Secondary School Emergency Relief Fund ("ESSER") monies allocated for American Indian students. From that amount, $4,000.00 was allocated to the IPAC. Whether any of the ESSER amount will be allocated to American Indian curriculum development is unknown. Indian curriculum development should be a CCSD priority given § 22-1-104 and the findings in 2018 of the U.S. Civil Rights Commission.[8] Also $4,000.00 of state funding was allocated to the IPAC.

At the CCSD BOE/ District Leadership Team Study Session on September 10, 2021, the CCSD acknowledged that if curriculum development is needed in a specific area, additional funding must be provided. Assistant Superintendent Giles said if the IPAC wanted Indian curriculum funding it would have to come out of the $8,000 and be voted on by IPAC.

March 26, 2021, IPAC Member Second CORA Request

A second CORA request was submitted to the CCSD for a response on (1) how is the District implementing § 22-1-104(1); and (2) provide any of the District's high school curriculum demonstrating implementation of § 22-1-104(1) and when the curriculum was implemented.

March 31, 2021, CCSD - No Timeframe in § 22-1-104 for Compliance

The CCSD responded that in the P.A.S.S. meetings it shared "that CCSD is in the process of updating its curriculum review process and timeline to satisfy the requirements of C.R.S. § 22-1-104." No documentation was provided by the CCSD regarding curriculum. Further, the CCSD was waiting to receive CO DOE "guidance as part of its process." Further, it is not out of compliance as "the statute does not establish a timeframe for when all the referenced topics should be incorporated into the civics curriculum."

April 2, 2021, CCSD's Second CORA Response – Ten Links to Web Sites

In its CORA response on April 13, 2021, the CCSD stated "it is presently including history, culture and contributions in its curriculum." The CCSD did not provide any curricular material in response, though they did supply a list of ten links to alleged curriculum resources provided to teachers. It is unknown if the CCSD's teachers actually utilize any of the links or any of the materials within each link. The focus of the materials in the links was not civic social contributions of minorities identified in § 22-1-104.

One link is called "Street Law," which is specific to court cases involving the First, Second, and Fourth Amendments of the United States Constitution. The content on the website literally fails to provide any content as required under § 22-1-104(1). There are no references to Colorado's African-American, Latin, Asian or LGBTQ communities. The Native American references included are only on how to get into law school.

A second link is called "National History Day," which is a nonprofit organization involving original research on historical topics of interest. The website fails to provide any content as required under § 22-1-104(1).

A third link is called "DBQ Project," which is about document based questions. The website fails to provide any content as required under § 22-1-104(1). The DBQ Project is unapologetically a writing program that also teaches history.

The fourth link is called "Teaching with Primary Sources." The website appears to teach students how to use primary sources. It does not include any content as required under § 22-1-104(1).

The fifth link is called the "Stanford History Education Group." The website involves teaching educators how to teach history. The website fails to provide any content as required under § 22-1-104(1).

The sixth link is called "1619," which focuses on American slavery. The website fails to address contributions of Colorado African-Americans or the contributions of other minority groups as identified in § 22-1-104(1).

The seventh link is called "Learning for Justice," which fails to provide any materials involving the history, culture, or contributions of those Coloradans who are within those minority groups as identified in § 22-1-104(1).

The eighth link is called "Native Knowledge 360," which is a teaching guide for educators concerning indigenous peoples in the Americas.

The ninth link is called "Resources," which is merely a link to other teaching resources. The website fails to provide any content as required under § 22-1-104(1).

The tenth link is a series of links to Schoology, which provides access to: 1) a newsletter for the CCSD Social Studies Teachers; and 2) High School US History and High School Government folders that are devoid of any content.

None of the links provided by the CCSD provided any materials involving Colorado minorities, or the Lesbian, Gay, Bisexual and Transgender individuals within these minority groups, and the intersectionality of significant social and cultural features within these communities as required under § 22-1-104(1).

May 2021, IPAC Member Meeting with CCSD

The CCSD reiterated its position in a meeting with the Indian Parent: (1) that it was waiting for guidance from the CO DOE; (2) it was in the process of updating its curriculum review process; and (3) the statute does not establish a timeframe for when all the referenced topics should be incorporated into the civics curriculum. They did agree that they did not have to hold a community forum which they said was satisfied by the ongoing communication with parents.

NOTES:

1. https://www.cherrycreekschools.org/Page/4015 (accessed online April 8, 2021).

2. https://www.cherrycreekschools.org/Page/13377 (accessed online April 8, 2021).

3. Grandview High School Registration Guide https://www.cherrycreekschools.org/site/handlers/filedownload.ashx?moduleinstanceid=9320&dataid=28994&FileName=Registration%20Guide%2020-21.pdf; no content references to Indian, Asian, gay, lesbian, bisexual, transgender, queer, and one each to Latino(a) [Latin American in Advanced Placement Spanish Literature and culture course] and African American [Concurrent Enrollment Survey of African-American Literature]. (accessed online February 8, 2021).

PART 21 / Colorado Education Associations and CCSD Lobbying

Colorado Education Association ("CEA") Supports C.R.S. § § 22-1-104 (1)-(6) (aka HB 19-1192)

CEA supports culturally relevant curriculum and supports the inclusion of local voices of community, parents, and educators in providing input and guidance in the decisions made in schools and districts.[1]

Colorado Association of School Boards ("CASB") Legal Opinion – Not Clear § 22-1-104 Constitutional

It may be that school districts are relying on the legal opinion of the CASB, dated May 2, 2018, in a letter sent to the CO DOE by Jenna Zerylnick, Legal Counsel for CASB:

> State law contains a civics requirement, though it does not mandate an assessment method for civics competency. C.R.S. § 22-1-104(3)(a) provides: "Satisfactory completion of a course on the civil government of the United States and the state of Colorado. which includes the subjects described in subsection (2) of this section, shall be a condition of high school graduation in the public schools of this state."
>
> ... Notably, the civics statute does not grant rulemaking authority to the State Board.
>
> Further, it is not clear that the civics statute is constitutional, as it mandates that all public schools in the state teach certain topics and information. The issue has not been litigated. However, even if the civics statute were constitutional, under this statute, local school boards still retain control over instruction, curriculum and assessment methods.
>
> Regardless of the constitutionality of the statute, the statute does not mandate an assessment method for civics competency nor does it grant rulemaking authority permitting the State Board to do so."

Signed: Ken DeLay, Executive Director, Colorado Association of School Boards

Michelle Murphy, Executive Director, Colorado Rural Schools Alliance[2]

This is in direct contradiction of the 1983 Colorado Attorney General Opinion, 983 Colo. AG LEXIS 33 (Dec. 2, 1983), and the *Skipworth v. Board of Educ.*, 874 P. Ed. 487 (1994) case.

CASB's Policy on Graduation Requirements - Recommended Language for CO School Districts that Best Meets Intent of Law, includes § 22-1-104(2) Civics Course

However, its current Policy on Graduation Requirements includes § 22-1-104.

> *"NOTE: State law requires all students to satisfactorily complete a course on the civil government of the State of Colorado and the United States (civics). C.R.S. 22-1-104. The Board has discretion to determine how the subject areas specified in C.R.S. 22-1-104, as well as the number of required credits, will be addressed when establishing graduation requirements for civics."*
>
> *NOTE: A local board may choose to require students to complete specific courses as part of its graduation requirements and identify them here. Please note that state law requires all students to satisfactorily complete a course on the civil government of the State of Colorado and the United States (civics). C.R.S. 22-1-104*[3]

CASB, Colorado Association of School Executives ("CASE") and CEA Joint Influence over Legislature and CO DOE

Ken Delay, CASB's executive director, said summit input will be very helpful in developing joint positions with the other associations on ESSA rules and regulations to take up with the State Board and in the General Assembly when legislators take up ESSA implementation in January. "If you haven't been there, you can't appreciate how much power there is in the Colorado Legislature when CASE, CEA and CASB all show up and say the same thing. It's a big deal."[4]

CCSD Lobbying

Many large school districts have their own lobbyists, with the suburban CCSD leading the pack in spending.

NOTES:

1. http://scorecard.coloradoea.org/2019/bills/hb-19-1192/ (accessed online January 5, 2021).

2. Letter from the Colorado Association of School Boards ("CASB") to the CO DOE, dated May 2, 2018, CDE Records https://go.boarddocs.com/co/cde/Board.nsf/files/AYLJUG4CF82E/$file/Public%20letters%20on%20ss%20standards.pdf (accessed online January 5, 2021).

3. CASB IKF Policy https://z2.ctspublish.com/casb/DocViewer.jsp?doccode=z20000254&z2collection=core (accessed online January 5, 2021).

4. https://ceawhatworks.wordpress.com/category/public-education/, June 2016 (accessed online March 1, 2021).

PART 22 / Colorado High School Diplomas; No Satisfactory Completion of Civil Government Course Required to Graduate, Including History, Culture and Social Contributions of American Indians

Academic Degrees Certify Students' Achievement

Academic degrees are a certification to the world at large of the recipient's educational achievement and fulfillment of the institution's standards. In addressing this issue, the Colorado Supreme Court in a case involving a Colorado high school in Durango, Colorado (*Department of Institutions ex rel. G. v. Bushnell*, 579 P.2d 1168 (1978)) upheld a refusal to grant a diploma to a student on the grounds that certain Durango High School graduation requirements had not been met. The court held that if a student has not actually satisfied substantive degree requirements the degree conferring entity would be in the position of making a false certification to the public at large of the accomplishment of persons who in fact lack the very qualifications. Such a [false certification] would undermine public confidence in the integrity of degrees, call academic standards into question, and harm those who rely on the certification which the degree represents.

Colorado's Tainted Diplomas - No Satisfactory Completion of Civil Government Course Required to Graduate, Including History, Culture and Social Contributions of American Indians

Even though the state legislature in 2003 made the completion of a course including these subjects a condition of graduation, school districts are willfully ignoring § 22-1-104. Students are receiving diplomas even if they have not been offered or satisfactorily completed the course required under § 22-1-104.

Revocation of Diplomas

In a 1992 10th Circuit Court of Appeals case regarding a university diploma issued in New Mexico, the court held that if a student did not complete the graduation requirements for a diploma and the diploma had already been delivered, it could still be revoked. See *Hand v. Matchett*, 957 F.2d 791, 794 (10th Cir. 1992).

Loss of Accreditation for Failure to Comply with Statutory and Regulatory Requirements

There are consequences for violating the state education statutes and regulatory directives which are very serious. These may include:

> When a school loses their accreditation, they may lose out on federal and state funding.
> A college or university may not recognize a diploma or credits (e.g., AP classes, concurrent enrollment) from an unaccredited high school.
> Students could be denied admission to colleges and universities and/or may be required to take remedial courses to make sure they are on track.
> Students may also be ineligible for scholarships when preparing for college.
> It may disqualify a student from receiving federal financial aid.
> It may impact military enlistments.[1]

NOTES:

1. Financial Impacts of Losing Accreditation https://www.collegesanddegrees.com/accreditation (accessed online February 10, 2021).

PART 23 / Federal Education Funding to State of Colorado for American Indian Students

Under various federal programs, the state of Colorado files applications to receive funding. They must comply with the funding requirements. One example for Colorado is its Report for Individuals with Disabilities Education Act ("IDEA") funding. The IDEA funding the state receives is second in amount of monies received from the federal government. Colorado's Report stated specifically that the state's course and graduation requirements under § 22-1-104 are a condition of graduation.[1]

State Performance Plan / Annual Performance Report: Part B for STATE FORMULA GRANT PROGRAMS under the Individuals with Disabilities Education Act. For reporting on FFY18, Colorado included the state course requirement under § 22-1-104 CRS as a condition of graduation.

Individuals with Disabilities Education Act Colorado Department of Education Performance Plan PART B, P. 7 , www.cde.state.co.us/cdesped/spp-apr

> Provide a narrative that describes the conditions youth must meet in order to graduate with a regular high school diploma and, if different, the conditions that youth with IEPs must meet in order to graduate with a regular high school diploma. If there is a difference, explain.
>
> Under Colorado law, "each school district board of education retains the authority to develop its own unique high school graduation requirements, so long as those local high school graduation requirements meet or exceed any minimum standards or basic core competencies or skills identified in the comprehensive set of guidelines for high school graduation developed by the state board pursuant to this paragraph." 22-2-106(1)(a.5) C.R.S. There are no specific courses, or numbers of courses, required by the state's graduation guidelines, and there are no legislated course requirements other than one course in Civics: "Satisfactory completion of a course on the civil government of the United States and the state of Colorado . . . shall be a condition of high school graduation in the public schools of this state." 22-1-104 (3)(a) C.R.S. Youth with IEPs must meet the same requirements as youth without IEPs in order to graduate with a regular high school diploma.

If Colorado is receiving any of this funding, it is obligated to address American Indian student needs, including the "lack of appropriate cultural awareness in school curriculum focusing on Native American history or culture" given the Findings of the Commission that this omission can (1) be harmful to American Indian students; (2) contribute to a negative learning environment; (3) be isolating and limiting; (4) trigger bullying; and (5) result in negative stereotypes across the board.

United States Department of Education ("US DOE") Must Investigate Use of Federal Funding Given to Colorado for American Indian Students

The majority of K-12 schools in the U.S. receive a combination of funds from local, state, and federal funding streams.[2] Title VI of the Elementary and Secondary Education Act ("ESEA") provides grants to support schools and school programs that serve Native American students. 20 U.S.C. §§ 7421–7429.[3]

The Chart below documents Funding for Native American Education:[4]

APPENDIX E: FUNDING FOR NATIVE AMERICAN EDUCATION

Department of the Interior Bureau of Indian Education									
Subactivity and Program Element (Amounts in $000s)	2011	2012	2013	2014	2015	2016	2017	2018 CR	2019 Request
Elementary and Secondary (forward funded)	520,048	522,247	524,205	518,318	536,897	553,458	575,155	571,250	511,788
ISEP Formula Funds	390,361	390,707	391,749	384,404	386,565	391,837	400,223	397,506	378,055
ISEP Program Adjustments	33,331	5,278	5,332	5,234	5,353	5,401	5,412	5,375	2,617
Education Program Enhancements	12,043	12,032	12,134	12,090	12,119	12,182	12,201	12,118	6,341
Tribal Education Departments (TEDs)					2,000	2,000	2,500	2,483	
Student Transportation	52,692	52,632	52,977	52,796	52,945	53,142	55,995	55,615	50,802
Early Child and Family Development	15,341	15,345	15,477	15,451	15,540	15,620	18,659	18,532	
Tribal Grant Support Costs	46,280	46,253	46,536	48,253	62,395	73,276	80,165	79,621	73,973
Elementary/Secondary Programs	76,939	122,534	123,591	118,402	119,195	134,263	140,540	139,586	114,128
Facilities Operations	59,149	58,565	58,982	55,668	55,865	63,098	66,219	65,769	60,405
Facilities Maintenance		50,665	51,213	48,396	48,591	55,887	59,043	58,642	53,723
Johnson-O'Malley Assistance Grants	13,416	13,304	13,396	14,338	14,739	14,778	14,778	14,678	
Residential Education Placement Programs	3,755								
Juvenile Detention Education	619					500	500	497	
Post Secondary Programs (forward funded)	64,192	67,293	68,943	69,793	69,793	74,893	77,207	76,683	72,128
Tribal Colleges and Universities (forward funded)	64,192	67,293	68,943	69,793	69,793	69,793	69,793	69,319	65,664
Post Secondary Programs	61,603	61,435	62,506	61,887	64,182	64,602	63,561	63,130	20,524
Education Management	29,916	21,971	21,539	20,354	20,464	25,151	35,050	34,812	23,282
Education Program Management	22,758	15,288	14,881	14,080	14,186	16,868	24,763	24,595	15,575
Education IT	7,158	6,683	6,658	6,274	6,278	8,283	10,287	10,217	7,707
Total	752,698	795,480	800,784	788,754	810,531	852,367	891,513	885,461	741,850
Department of the Interior Education Construction									
Replacement School Construction	21,463	17,807	17,807	954	20,165	45,504	45,504	45,195	
Replacement Facility Construction	29,466					11,935	11,935	11,854	
Employee Housing Repair	4,438	4,428	4,442	3,818	3,823	7,565	7,567	7,516	5,060
Facilities Improvement and Repair	85,142	48,591	48,777	50,513	50,513	73,241	68,251	67,788	67,791
Total – Education Construction	140,509	70,826	71,026	55,285	74,501	138,245	133,257	132,353	72,851

Source: Department of the Interior, Bureau of Indian Affairs

The need for auditing how Indian federal funds are spent can be seen in the National Advisory Council on Indian Education ("NACIE") caution. NACIE was concerned whether "Title VI funds go specifically toward the Indian students and tribal communities for whom they are intended and that services continue to target the unique, culturally related academic needs of [American Indian/ Alaskan Native] ("AIAN") students. NACIE is concerned that budgeted and unfilled vacancies at the U.S. Department of Education ("ED") and Office of Indian Education ("OIE") have reduced the capacity to monitor all ESEA* grant programs to ensure that Title funds are spent appropriately."[5]

* Elementary and Secondary Education Act of 1965 (ESEA) as amended by the Every Student Succeeds Act (ESSA), 20 U.S.C. §7471.

When signed into law in 2015, ESSA further advanced equity in U.S. education policy by upholding important protections outlined in "No Child Left Behind" (NCLB). At the same time, it granted flexibility to states in exchange for rigorous and comprehensive state-developed plans designed to close achievement gaps, increase equity, improve the quality of instruction, and increase outcomes for all students.[6]

The chart below details New Mexico's allocation of Indian education:[7]

District Funding 2019–2020: Operating Budget Estimated Revenue

District	Total District Budget	25184 Indian Ed Formula Grant	25147 Impact Aid Indian Education	25131 Johnson O'Malley	27150 Indian Education Act
Albuquerque	1,435,693,501	0	7,379	0	90,000
Aztec	50,521,246	0		33,568	64,000
Bernalillo	69,875,709	238,340	1,733,488		90,000
Bloomfield	55,472,141	219,175	338,971	78,241	52,200
Central	111,625,163	1,215,514	10,316,875	327,119	60,000
Cuba	15,968,451	69,432	484,168	37,216	90,000
DEAP	489,808				74,540
Dream Diné	806,967				67,301
Dulce	23,701,991		1,453,675		47,907
Española	54,419,157		30,692		83,909
Farmington	151,878,146	295,852	34,463	295,852	55,203.78
Gallup	232,536,693		17,751,517		90,000
Grants/Cibola	69,125,373		1,230,477		90,000
Hozho Academy	1,264,927				90,000
Jemez Mountain	5,967,901	134,478	134,478		25,000
Jemez Valley	11,628,497	542,920	542,920		50,000
Los Lunas	125,708,997	166,404	166,404		
Magdalena	7,775,580	133,017	133,017		80,232
NACA	5,635,504				90,000
Peñasco	7,042,572	6,826	6,826	0	85,263.18
Pojoaque Valley	27,343,701	957,428	957,428		90,000
Rio Rancho	278,783,521				54,950
Ruidoso	45,014,068	145,787	145,787		50,000
San Diego Riverside Charter	1,734,739	163,631	163,631		90,000
Santa Fe	345,395,204				89,658
Six Directions Indigenous	1,484,471	25,130			90,000
Taos	39,040,757	90,793	25,130		90,766
Tularosa	18,551,183	283,226	90,793		0
Walatowa Charter High School	3,113,171	2,625,677	283,226	0	50,000
Zuni	26,147,665	25,130	2,625,677	215,674	36,441
GRAND TOTAL	**5,953,349,845**	**5,270,934**	**38,658,302.00**	**987,670**	**2,017,370.96**

Example of Need for US DOE Audit

In 2011, Jose Esquibel with the Colorado Department of Public Health and Environment ("CO DPHE") and Carol Harvey, Executive Secretary, Colorado Commission of Indian Affairs, requested a meeting with U.S. Health and Human Services ("US HHS") Regional Director Marguerite Salazar to discuss federal health funding given to states with an expectation that a portion of that funding go to American Indian tribes and urban and other health organizations serving American Indians. In 2011, the State had no way to break out funding to allocate to Indian health organizations. For example, the state would receive federal funding for cancer, diabetes, mental health or alcoholism with a portion earmarked for American Indians. Yet the state had no way to allocate the portion earmarked for American Indians. The state provided a letter to US HHS Regional Director Salazar to avoid any liability on its part for its failure to make this allocation. The state, in September 2021, confirmed this continues to be the case.

U.S. Department of the Interior, Office of Natural Resources Revenue ("ONNR")

If Colorado is found to have improperly allocated or used funding for American Indian students, it must perform a restructured accounting. One area in which the federal government has successfully used restructured accounting is in the area of the payment of royalties under federal and Indian oil and gas leases.

ONRR has the statutory authority to issue orders to perform a restructured accounting when it discovers that a lessee made incorrect royalty payments based upon *repeated, systemic reporting errors.* To issue an order for a restructured accounting, ONRR must find that the lessee has made identified underpayments or overpayments based upon repeated, systemic reporting errors for a significant number of leases or a single lease for a significant number of reporting months. These repeated, systemic reporting errors must constitute a pattern of violations that are likely to result in significant underpayments or overpayments.

If either Colorado self-reports or the US DOE discovers that Colorado has improperly allocated or wrongfully used funding for the education of American Indian students, Colorado must perform a restructured accounting and repay funds misused, with interest. As this area involves American Indians, there is no statute of limitations defense, and it is incumbent upon the US DOE to act given the federal government's fiduciary relationship that must be honored.

NOTES:

1. IDEA CO DOE Performance Plan https://www.cde.state.co.us/cdesped/spp-aprion (accessed online March 5, 2021).

2. U.S. Civil Rights Commission, December 2018 Report "Broken Promises: Continuing Federal Funding Shortfall for Native Americans, p. 109. https://www.usccr.gov/files/pubs/2018/12-20-Broken-Promises.pdf (accessed online September 5, 2021).

3. Ibid., p. 110.

4. Ibid., p. 269.

5. https://oese.ed.gov/files/2021/02/2020AnnualReport_I_12072020.pdf, p. 13 (accessed online September 5, 2021).

6. https://www.casb.org/what-you-need-to-know-about-the-misuse-of-crt (accessed online September 5, 2021).

7. https://webnew.ped.state.nm.us/wp-content/uploads/2021/01/TESR2020.pdf (accessed online September 5, 2021).

PART 24 / Investigation of Colorado Public School Districts, including Cherry Creek School District, to Determine if There Is a Countenanced, Systemic Violation by High Schools of § 22-1-104, C.R.S. - No Satisfactory Completion of Civil Government Course Required to Graduate, Including History, Culture and Social Contributions of American Indians

Petition for Investigation of Colorado Public School Districts, including Cherry Creek School District, to Determine if There Is a Countenanced, Systemic Violation by High Schools of § 22-1-104, C.R.S.

On August 13, 2021, the Petition below was submitted to Colorado Governor Polis:

> **Forty-eight years ago, the Colorado legislature mandated public school instruction about Spanish Americans and Negroes (C.R.S. 1973, §123-21-4). Twenty-five years ago, under the persistent leadership of Cherokee [should be Comanche] State Senator Suzanne Williams, American Indians were added (1998, HB 1186). Eighteen years ago, the legislature added the satisfactory completion of a civil government course as a condition of high school graduation, which included instruction about the history, culture and contributions of African and Hispanic Americans and American Indians, starting in Two Thousand Seven (SB 36). In 2019, Asian-Americans, LGBTQ individuals and religious minorities were added, with immediate effect (HB 19-1192), which you signed in a symbolic ceremony at Rudolfo "Corky" Gonzales Branch Library.**
>
> Required compliance with this statute, § 22-1-104, C.R.S., is repeatedly stated on the Colorado Department of Education's ("CDE") website. **The CDE's 2018 Report to the U.S. Department of Education on federal funding** for Individuals with Disabilities specifically cites § 22-1-104's course and graduation requirements. The Colorado Attorney General in 1983 and the judiciary in 1994 upheld § 22-1-104. A federal case, cited

§ 22-1-104, in *dicta*, as an example of a valid curriculum requirement, in which Cherry Creek was a defendant.

Cherry Creek's Graduation Requirements, promulgated unanimously by its Board in 2016, 2018 and 2020, cite § 22-1-104(3)(a) and its "civil government graduation requirement." At a **February 8, 2021, meeting with Cherry Creek's Indigenous Parent Action Committee**, former Superintendent Siegfried acknowledged a § 22-1-104 course isn't offered, but the content is covered in other courses which is enough to satisfy § 22-1-104. By federal and state law, course completion, not content, must be reported to assure civil rights compliance. **Minority students expressed their concerns regarding Grandview High School's curriculum in the attached article.** Grandview is in the Cherry Creek School District. Records provided in December 2020, pursuant to a Colorado Open Records Act, provided no evidence of a § 22-1-104 course. If Cherry Creek isn't complying with § 22-1-104, it must **report its non-compliance** to the CDE or be in breach of its contract filed with the CDE, assuring Cherry Creek's compliance with all applicable statutory requirements. It alleges it is revising its curriculum but there is no reference to § 22-1-104. This revision is scheduled for implementation in four more years or longer. To comply with CDE's 2020 Civics Standards and House Bill 19-1192, Jefferson County's School District updated its Civics Units of Study on February 26, 2020.

Numerous Internet sites address § 22-1-104, including the Education Commission of the States, which may be publicly misleading and detrimental to the state's reputation and integrity.

As statewide compliance with § 22-1-104 is questionable, the state must determine if there is a **countenanced, systemic violation of § 22-1-104** ongoing which could **impact** (1) public schools' accreditation; (2) federal funding; (3) the legally protected classes under § 22-1-104; (4) the constitutionally protected property interest of students to a valid diploma; and (5) public safety, given the militia's chilling engagement at Cherry Creek's Board meeting on June 23, 2021. Over 100 persons spoke at the meeting on curriculum review, with many more in attendance.

Attachment

Individuals with Disabilities Education Act Colorado Department of Education Performance Plan PART B, P. 7, www.cde.state.co.us/cdesped/spp-apr

Provide a narrative that describes the conditions youth must meet in order to graduate with a regular high school diploma and, if different, the conditions that youth with IEPs must meet in order to graduate with a regular high school diploma. If there is a difference, explain.

Under Colorado law, "each school district board of education retains the authority to develop its own unique high school graduation requirements, so long as those local high school graduation requirements meet or exceed any minimum standards or basic core competencies or skills identified in the comprehensive set of guidelines for high school graduation developed by the state board pursuant to this paragraph." 22-2-106(1)(a.5) C.R.S. There are no specific courses, or numbers of courses, required by the state's graduation guidelines, and there are no legislated course requirements other than one course in Civics: "Satisfactory completion of a course on the civil government of the United States and the state of Colorado . . . shall be a condition of high school graduation in the public schools of this state." 22-1-104 (3)(a) C.R.S. Youth with IEPs must meet the same requirements as youth without IEPs in order to graduate with a regular high school diploma.

ATTORNEY GENERAL AND STATE AND FEDERAL CASE CITES

1983 CO Attorney General Opinion 983 Colo. AG LEXIS 33 (Dec. 2, 1983)

Skipworth v. Board of Educ., 874 P. Ed. 487 (1994)

Lane v. Owens, U.S. District Court of Colorado, Civil Docket Case No 1:03-cv-01544-LTB, Judge Lewis T. Babcock, August 15, 2003, Ruling (pp. 6-7)

JEFFCO Social Studies Curriculum Update

https://www.thepulsefromcandi.com/blog/category/socialstudies

To comply with CDE's Two Thousand Twenty (2020) Civics Standards and House Bill 19-1192, Jefferson County's School District updated its Civics Units of Study in February Two Thousand Twenty (2020).

INTERNET CITES of § 22-1-104

"Colorado in particular has one of the most robust civics education requirements in the country. In fact, the only statewide graduation requirement in Colorado is the completion of a civics and government course. Colorado designed curriculum for a full year civics course, and provides a myriad of resources and guidance for teachers on the subject." https://populationeducation.org/an-essential-guide-to-civics-education-in-the-united-states-today/

Education Commission of the States Colorado: Public schools are required to teach a course on the history and civil government of the state of Colorado and the United States, to include the history, culture and contributions of minorities. Satisfactory completion of this course is required for high school graduation. C.R.S. 22-1-104

https://www.csmonitor.com/Media/Content/2018/0323/0323-civics-map

https://www.edweek.org/teaching-learning/data-most-states-require-history-but-not-civics

https://ecs.secure.force.com/mbdata/MBQuest2RTANW?Rep=CIP1601S

https://www.americanprogress.org/issues/education-k-12/reports/2018/02/21/446857/state-civics-education/

https://www.aft.org/ae/summer2018/shapiro_brown

https://medium.com/generation-citizen/mapping-the-civic-education-policy-landscape-9e5766692efe

The March 9, 2021, Curriculum Equity article in the Grandview High School Chronicle was also attached.

The following parties were copied on the Petition: Office of Colorado Attorney General Philip J. Weiser, Colorado Department of Education, Commissioner of Education Katy Anthes, PhD, Cherry Creek School District Board of Education, President Joseph Biden, U.S. Department of Education, Secretary Dr. Miguel Cardona, U.S. Department of Justice—Civil Rights, Assistant Attorney General Kristen Clarke, along with various state legislators, minority support groups, and media outlets.

On August 13, 2021, the U.S. Department of Justice—Office of Civil Rights responded immediately, as did Colorado State Representative Brianna Titone, HD27. Also, Rep. Herod's office has promptly responded to all of my emails.

On August 25, 2021, a United States Attorney's Office Call Request email was received for more information in order to determine whether to open an investigation.

Protest Commenced August 19, 2021 - No Satisfactory Completion of Civil Government Course Required to Graduate, Including History, Culture and Social Contributions of American Indians

Starting on August 19, 2021, Carol Harvey, commenced a march at the Colorado State Capitol. She will march alone in front of the Capitol building in downtown Denver for one hour a day, three days a week. This march will continue until the later of (1) Governor Polis issuing an order for Colorado public schools to comply with § 22-1-104; or (2) the CCSD complying with the § 22-1-104 course and graduation requirement. It is a moral and sacred commitment. As a Navajo Nation citizen, her ancestors were "forced marched" as "prisoners-of-war" the one-way 300-mile distance from their home to the site of their five-year imprisonment at Fort Sumner, New Mexico, during the Navajo-American War. It will be a time of solitude and isolation.

As Gandhi stated: "A 'No' uttered from the deepest conviction is better than a 'Yes' merely uttered to please, or worse, to avoid trouble."[1]

New Mexico Federal Case - *Yazzie-Martinez v. State of New Mexico*: State's Public Education Department Failed to Provide Native American, Hispanic and Other Students from Diverse Populations a Sufficient Education Due in Part To Lack of Culturally and Linguistically Relevant Curriculum

The Navajo Times reported on the "Protecting the Sacred Trust" press conference, which in part concerned the delay in culturally and linguistically relevant curriculum development in New Mexico and much more, conveying the sacredness of the Indians' purpose.

Wilhelmina Yazzie, the lead New Mexico Navajo plaintiff in the *Yazzie-Martinez v. State of New Mexico* lawsuit echoed the concerns of parents: "Our children are starved for equal opportunity in education, most of all culturally relevant education." Wilhelmina Yazzie's eldest son was a fourth grader when she became a plaintiff in the landmark lawsuit that found the state's public education system failed to provide several groups of at-risk students an adequate education. He graduated from high school in Gallup this year.

> "This is not about politics," he said, "this is a deeper spiritual act of doing what is required of us. "We were given the sacred trust to be the guardian and protectors of all the gifts of our creator, the most precious of those are our children and our elders," he said.
>
> Judge Singleton found that the state's Public Education Department fails to provide Native American, Hispanic and other students from diverse populations a sufficient education due in part to a lack of culturally and linguistically relevant curriculum. ... "When children of color do not see themselves reflected in a positive light in school curriculum, they are less likely to be engaged and less likely believe they can succeed," said James Jimenez, New Mexico Voices for Children executive director. ... The court's ruling made it clear that Native children have a constitutional right to a culturally responsive education," stated Sanchez. ... "In order to meaningfully address and eliminate the systemic racism that is present within New Mexico's educational system, it is imperative that the state take greater action in fulfilling its obligations as outlined by the landmark *Yazzie-Martinez v. State of New Mexico*.[2]

On June 29, 2021, New Mexico Governor Lujan-Grisham tried unsuccessfully to get the lawsuit dismissed. First Judicial District Court Judge Matthew Wilson noted that "the state, by its own admission, is not fulfilling its constitutional duty to provide a sufficient education to all students." The judge stated, "The state cannot be deemed to have complied with this court's order until it shows that the necessary programs and reforms are being provided to all at risk students to ensure that they have the opportunity to be college and career ready." This case involved a monumental discovery effort. The cost and time-consuming process in litigation are flaws in the judicial system. [3]

On August 24, 2021, the New Mexico Department of Education issued a Draft Plan which was found to be short on substance.[4]

Email from Governor Polis, September 16, 2021 – No Response on § 22-1-104

I received a form Email from Governor Polis on September 16, 2021. I thanked the sender but I stated that the Email did not address my Petition or Protest.

NOTES:

1. https://www.biography.com/news/gandhi-quotes (accessed online September 19, 2021).

2. https://navajotimes.com/reznews/calls-continue-for-top-aide-to-step-down/ (accessed online August 24, 2021).

3. http://nmpovertylaw.org/tag/yazzie-v-state-of-new-mexico/ (accessed online September 6, 2021).

4. https://www.usnews.com/news/best-states/new-mexico/articles/2021-08-24/document-hints-t-solving-new-mexico-education-inadequacies (accessed online September 6, 2021).

PART 25 / Brief Review of Indian History Policy

In reviewing the Reports of the Commissioners of Indian Affairs to the Secretary of the Interior from 1855 to 1888 in regard to the area which would later become the state of Colorado, the troubling history revealed is important to all students. The cost benefit analysis of the extermination of all Indians in the United States is part of the legacy of Indian peoples. By 1859, the United States had essentially deprived the Indians living in or hunting and gathering or visiting spiritual sites in the Colorado area of any means of traditional subsistence. This led to Indians either plundering for survival or starvation. Predominating at the highest levels of government were stereotypes of Indians focused year after year on their paganism, debauchery, indolence and their lack of regard for women. The policy of removal, the imperative of assimilation versus outright extermination, the ever-westward movement of settlers without regard for Indian land rights, the confiscation of land at bargain basement prices for homesteading and railroads, and the trespass on Indian reservations for valuable minerals, timber and agricultural, arable land is reported year after year as part of our history.

Stereotypical View of Indians Expressed at Highest Levels of Government

John N. Oberly, Commissioner of Indian Affairs, in his Annual Report to the Secretary of the Interior in 1888, wrote the following:

> The Indian has indeed begun to change with the changing times. He is commencing to appreciate the fact that he must become civilized-must, as he expresses it, "learn the white man's way" - or perish from the face of the earth. He can not sweep back with a broom the flowing tide. The forests into which he ran whooping from the door of "William and Mary" have been felled. The game on which he lived has disappeared. The war-path has been obliterated. He is hemmed in on all sides by white population. The railroad

refuses to be excluded from his reservation-that hot-bed of barbarism, in which many noxious social and political weeds grow rankly. The Christian missionary is persistently entreating him to abandon paganism. Gradually the paternal hand of the Government is being withdrawn from his support. His environments no longer compel him, or afford to him opportunities, to display the nobler traits of his character. On the warpath and in the chase he was heroic: all activity; patient of hunger; patient of fatigue; coolheaded-a creature of exalted fortitude. "But," says a writer, sketching his character, "when the chase was over, when the war was done, and the peacepipes smoked out, he abandoned himself to debauchery and idleness. To sleep all day in a wigwam of painted skins, filthy and blackened with smoke, adorned with scalps, and hung with tomahawks and arrows, to dance in the shine of the new moon to music made from the skin of snakes, to tell stories of witches and evil spirits, to gamble, to sing, to jest, to boast of his achievements in war, and to sit with a solemn gravity at the councils of his chiefs constituted his most serious employment. His squaw was his slave. With no more affection than a coyote feels for its mate, he brought her to his wigwam that she might gratify the basest of his passions and minister to his wants. It was Starlight or Cooing Dove that brought the wood for his fire and the water for his drink, that plowed the field and sowed the maize.[1]

These stereotypes became embedded in the consciousness of whites.

Extermination, Extinction or Starvation for Indians

As reported by several Commissioners of Indian Affairs to the Secretary of the Interior, Indians would either be exterminated by whites, become extinct or starve to death. One option proposed in 1858 was indentureship of Indian children to whites, which was akin to slavery.[2]

Annual Report of the Commissioner of Indian Affairs, Nov. 26, 1855: Indians Would Either Be Exterminated by Whites or Become Extinct

In the November 26, 1855 Annual Report of the Commissioner of Indian Affairs, Commissioner George W. Manypenny advised the Secretary of the Interior, who served on the President's Cabinet of the grave situation for Indians - "the obliteration of game had reduced the Indians to either stealing food for survival or starving. ... Indians would either be exterminated by the whites or become extinct."[3]

Annual Report of the Commissioner of Indian Affairs, Nov. 6, 1858: Allow Indians to Starve or Exterminate Them

In 1858, Commissioner Charles E. Fix reported that there was no land left on which a subsistence lifestyle could be possible. He alerted the Secretary of the Interior that "with the limited military force available to prevent Indian depredations the only alternatives were to allow the Indians to starve or exterminate them."[4]

Annual Report of the Commissioner of Indian Affairs, Nov. 1859: Gold Discoveries in Colorado; United States Deprived Indians of Any Means of Subsistence in Colorado

In November 1859, the Commissioner of Indian Affairs A. B. Greenwood informed the Secretary of the Interior that the United States had essentially deprived the Indians living in or hunting and gathering or visiting spiritual sites in the Colorado area of any means of traditional subsistence.

> A crisis has now, however, arrived in our relations with them. Since the discovery of gold in the vicinity of "Pike's Peak," the emigration has immensely increased; the Indians have been driven from their local haunts and hunting grounds, and the game so far killed off or dispersed, that it is now impossible for the Indians to obtain the necessary subsistence from that source. In fact, we have substantially taken possession of the country and deprived them of their accustomed means of support. ... They have also been brought to realize that a stern necessity is impending over them; that they cannot pursue their former mode of life, but must entirely change their habits, and, in fixed localities, look to the cultivation of the soil and the raising of stock for their future support. There is no alternative to providing for them in this manner but to exterminate them, which the dictates of justice and humanity alike forbid. They cannot remain as they are; for, if nothing is done for them, they must be subjected to starvation, or compelled to commence robbing and plundering for a subsistence.[5]

Annual Report of the Commissioner of Indian Affairs, 1862, Commissioner William P. Dole: Colorado and Washington Gold Rushes Infringing on Indian Rights[6]

Considerable difficulty has been created in Colorado and Washington with the tribes in those Territories by the great increase of immigration, attracted by newly discovered gold mines. The Indians claim that the land belongs to them, while the miners, in search of new veins, are disposed to pay but little respect to their claims. A sufficient extent of country should be assigned to the Indians, and they should be protected in its enjoyment.

Annual Report of the Commissioner of Indian Affairs, Oct. 1863 – Colorado Territory - Rich in Mineral Wealth; Ute Cession to United States of Arable Land and Mining Districts in Colorado[7]

Colorado Territory - Rich in Mineral Wealth, Containing Gold, Silver, Copper, Iron, Coal and Salt, Alabaster, Limestone, and Gypsum

> Colorado Territory, resting upon the headwaters of the Platte and Arkansas rivers and the western slope of the Rocky mountains, is rich in mineral wealth, containing gold, silver, copper, iron, coal and salt, alabaster, limestone, and gypsum. None but gold mines have been worked to any extent; these are proving remunerative ...

At the same time as Indians were compelled to starve or steal necessities in order to live, the federal government continued negotiations for cessions of large tracts of Indian land. One such cession in Colorado included land of the Tabeguache, or "People of Sun Mountain," one of the largest of the ten nomadic bands of the Ute. They lived in river valleys of the Gunnison River and Uncompahgre River and considered the Pikes Peak region their home.

In October 1863, Commissioner William P. Dole stressed the importance of the Treaty negotiated with the Tabequache band of Utahs extinguishing their title to white settlements in Colorado, and more importantly to valuable mining districts:

> It will be seen that by the treaty negotiated with the Tabequache band of Utahs, as above stated, the Indian title is extinguished to one among [sic] the largest and most valuable tracts of land ever ceded to the United States. It includes nearly all the important settlements thus far made in Colorado, and all the valuable mining districts discovered up to this time.

Annual Report of the Commissioner of Indian Affairs, 1864, Colorado Superintendency: Cheyennes and Arapahoes Want Peace - Military Says Further Chastisement Needed; Sand Creek Massacre[8]

Cheyennes and Arapahoes Want Peace - Military Says Further Chastisement Needed

> ... on the 4th of September Agent Colley forwarded to the superintendent a letter signed by several of the Cheyenne chiefs, proposing terms of peace. On the 28th an interview took place between Governor Evans and these chiefs, at which, it appears, from the annual report of that officer, they seemed earnest for peace; but the governor deemed it his duty, under the existing circumstances, to decline acceding to their terms, or indeed to make any terms with them, and the interview ended with leaving the chiefs referred to, or any others who might be disposed towards peace, to communicate with the military authorities. *This course seems, from the paper accompanying Governor Evans's report, to have commended itself to Major General Curtis as the proper one to be pursued, that officer deeming it necessary, in order to a permanent peace and the future good behavior of the Indians, that they should receive further punishment; ... Governor Evans advocates the policy of a winter expedition against the offending tribes.* (Emphasis added).

Sand Creek Massacre

The 'disastrous and shameful occurrence'—the Sand Creek Massacre—was reported:

> Most disastrous and shameful occurrence of all, the massacre of a large number of men, women and children of the Indians of this agency by the troops under command of Colonel Chivington, of the United States volunteer cavalry of Colorado. Several hundred of them had come in to a place designated by Governor Evans as a rendezvous for those who would separate themselves from the hostile parties, these Indians were set upon and butchered in cold blood by troops in the service of the United States.

Annual Report of the Commissioner of Indian Affairs, 1865: Metals Are Sole Reliance to Liquidate Interest on National Debt; Cost-Benefit Analysis of Total Destruction of Indians; Whip Cheyennes; Major Wyncoop with Chiefs of Tribes Under His Charge Met with Governor Evans, Colorado, Seeking Peace; Arapahoe and Cheyenne Indians who Escaped from Sand Creek Massacre - Left Almost Helpless in Dead of Winter; Treaty with

Arapahoes - No Money, No Specific Land; Commissioners Negotiating with Arapahoes for Treaty – Hard, Mean-Spirited, Sharp Negotiating Tactics Used by U.S., Give Land with Game and Arable Land, Not Gold and Silver[9]

Metals Are Sole Reliance to Liquidate Interest on National Debt

> The precious metals, our sole reliance to liquidate the accruing interest upon the national debt, are derived chiefly from the mining districts of Colorado, Oregon, California, Nevada, Idaho, and Montana, and any barrier which obstructs emigration to these mines, and retards their development, must prove highly prejudicial to the financial prosperity of the country.

Cost-Benefit Analysis of Total Destruction of Indians

In an Extract from the 1865 Commissioner of Indian Affairs Report to the Secretary of the Interior, we find the following cost-benefit analysis of the total destruction of the Indians:

> The policy of the total destruction of the Indians has been advocated by gentlemen of high position, intelligence, and personal character; but no enlightened nation can adopt or sanction it without a forfeiture of its self-respect and the respect of the civilized nations of the earth.
>
> Financial considerations forbid the inauguration of such a policy. The attempted destruction of three hundred thousand of these people, accustomed to a nomadic life, subsisting upon the spontaneous productions of the earth, and familiar with the fastnesses of the mountains and the swamps of the plains, would involve an appalling sacrifice of the lives of our soldiers and frontier settlers, and the expenditure of untold treasure. It is estimated that the maintenance of each regiment of troops engaged against the Indians of the plains costs the government two million dollars per annum. All the military operations of last summer have not occasioned the immediate destruction of more than a few hundred Indian warriors. Such a policy is manifestly as impracticable as it is in violation of every dictate of humanity and Christian duty.

Whip Cheyennes

> "...the Cheyennes will have to be roundly whipped—or completely

wiped out—before they will be quiet. I say that if any of them are caught in your vicinity, the only thing to do is kill them." A month later, while addressing a gathering of church deacons, he dismissed the possibility of making a treaty with the Cheyenne: "It simply is not possible for Indians to obey or even understand any treaty. I am fully satisfied, gentlemen, that to kill them is the only way we will ever have peace and quiet in Colorado." (Emphasis added.)

Major Wyncoop with Chiefs of Tribes Under His Charge Met with Governor Evans, Colorado, Seeking Peace

I have the honor to enclose herewith papers relating to the late massacre of friendly Indians by Colonel J.M. Chivington,* near Fort Lyon. It is impossible for me to express to you the horror with which I view this transaction; it has destroyed the last vestige of confidence between the red and white man. Nearly every one of the chiefs and headmen of the Arapahoe and Cheyenne tribes who had remained true to the whites, and were determined not to fight the whites, were cruelly murdered when resting in all the confidence of assurances from Major Wyncoop, and I also believe from Major Anthony, that they should not be disturbed. Major Wyncoop, of the Colorado cavalry, was doing all that it was possible for an officer to do to pacify the Indians, and had restored comparative peace to this frontier, when all his work was destroyed, and an Indian war inaugurated that must cost the government millions of money and thousands of lives. These are the bitter fruits of Governor Evans's proclamation that I sent you last summer - "to the victor belongs the spoils." I then stated that those men could not stop to inquire if the Indians they should come in contact with were friendly or hostile. When Major Wyncoop went to Denver with the chiefs of tribes under his charge, why did Governor Evans refuse to act in any way, for or against them ... they were determined not to fight the whites...Little Bear escaped with his band; and it is due to him and to humanity that no effort be spared, in my opinion, to save him and his from certain destruction. I'm making every effort possible to find the Comanches and Kiowas; but I have little hope of succeeding. J. H. Leaven Worth, U.S. Indian Agent

*The papers referred to above were not received.

Arapahoe and Cheyenne Indians who Escaped from Sand Creek Massacre - Left Almost Helpless in Dead of Winter

> [Arapahoes who escaped from the massacre of Sand creek.] These last came to me exceedingly poor having lost everything in that attack on them by Colonel Chivington; not only their horses, mules, and lodges, but all the tools they possessed; and were left almost helpless in the dead of winter. Their condition requires the most urgent attention of the department.

Treaty with Arapahoes, No Money, No Specific Land

Charles Mix, Acting Commissioner stated as follows:

> Agreements to pay money will not be approved. If a treaty is made, it will be one of occupancy only, no title to lands will be acknowledged in the Indians of the country they abandon, nor will any be conferred upon them in the country they are to inhabit; Just an article may be inserted providing that the whites will be excluded from settlement in the country assigned to them.

Commissioners Negotiating with Arapahoes for Treaty – Hard, Mean-Spirited, Sharp Negotiating Tactics Used by U.S., Give Land with Game and Arable Land, Not Gold and Silver

The Arapahoes didn't want to agree on land at the time—few were present, the rest were up north. They were still reeling from the Sand Creek Massacre:

> **Little Raven There is something very strong for us-that fool band of soldiers that cleared out our lodges, and killed our women and children. This is strong (hard) on us. There, at Sand creek, is one chief, Left Hand; White Antelope and many other chiefs lie there; our women and children lie there. Our lodges were destroyed there, and our horses were taken from us there, and I do not feel disposed to go right off in a new country and leave them. What I have to say, I am glad to see you writing it down to take to the Big Chief in Washington.** (Emphasis added).

Notwithstanding their need for more time, the Commissioners pressed them on anyway - *"We want to give you a country that is full of game and good for agricultural purposes, and where the hills and mountains are not full of gold and silver."*

We all fully realize that it is hard for any people to leave their homes and graves of their ancestors; but, **unfortunately for you, gold has been discovered in your country**, and a crowd of white people have gone there to live, and a great many of these people are the worst enemies of the Indians men who do not care for their interests, and who would not stop at any crime to enrich themselves. These men are now in your country - in all parts of it and there is no portion where you can live and maintain yourselves but what you will come in contact with them. The consequences of this state of things are that you are in constant danger of being imposed upon, and you have to resort to arms in self defence. Under the circumstances, there is, in the opinion of the commission, no part of the former country large enough where you can live at peace. The white men who are there do not regard law, and the President desires to punish them, yet it will not come until they have committed actual hostilities against the Indians.

Before the President can hear of their bad deeds a state of hostilities is created, and you are the sufferers. Under the circumstances the commissioners desire you to carefully consider whether it is not best for you to go to some other country where you will not be disturbed in this manner.

We want to give you a country that is full of game and good for agricultural purposes, and where the hills and mountains are not full of gold and silver. In such a country as this the government can fully provide for your wants
...

We believe that in the country where we desire you to go you will gradually become rich, and your numbers increase; but we are fully convinced that it is impossible for you to stay, and that if you do stay, you will gradually diminish, until you are finally swept from the earth.

We are sorry that we have bad people among us, as you are sorry that you have bad people among you; but this is unfortunately the case with all people, and however severe we make laws; it is impossible to prevent crime.

You may accede to our wishes, and be happy and prosperous, or you may refuse to make a treaty, and be ruined in health and happiness.

Wise and good men have for many years, at Washington, been studying what is best for Indians to do. They have arrived at the conclusion that it is best for the two races to be separated.

> From the earliest history of our country, where the white man has come in contact with the Indians, you have gradually wasted away from the earth; and for this reason they have concluded it best for the two races to be separated.
>
> The treaty which had been prepared was now read, article by article, by President Sanborn, and interpreted by John Smith to the Indians present. An article was submitted authorizing the Senate to make amendments without reference back to the Indians, but was objected to by the Indians, and withdrawn.
>
> The treaty was then signed by the commissioners and the chiefs and headmen of the Cheyenne and Arapaho tribes, and witnessed by the secretaries and other persons present, when the council adjourned John R. Sanborn. President of the Commission (Emphasis added.)

Annual Report of the Commissioner of Indian Affairs, 1866: Treaty with Utes – Gold, Silver and Coal Discovered on Their Land; Fertile Land, Timber, Water Power, All Requirements for Profitable Occupation; Limit Payment to Utes[10]

The Central Superintendency reported the following:

> Colorado Territory. Last summer gold, silver, and coal were discovered in this section, which is reported to have many fertile valleys, abundance of timber and water powers, a fine climate, and all the requirements for profitable occupation. Many parties are preparing to invade this new land early in the spring ... It is important that a treaty be made with the Grand River and Uintah bands at as early a day as possible. I need scarcely allude to the necessity of limiting, as far as possible, the amount which the government will be called upon to pay for a cession of the right of occupancy of the land by the Indians, but deem it of importance that, so far as possible, no promises of money annuities shall be made, but that all payments shall be made in stock animals, implements, goods adapted to their wants, and for other beneficial objects.

Annual Report of the Commissioner of Indian Affairs, 1877: Proposal to Remove Indians in Colorado and Arizona to Facilitate Gold and Silver Mining and Farming by Whites

In this connection, I recommend the removal of all the Indians in Colorado and Arizona to the Indian Territory. In Colorado, gold and silver mines are scattered over a wide extent of territory, and are to be found in every conceivable direction, running into Indian reservations. Of course miners will follow the various leads and prospect new ones without regard to the barriers set up by an Indian reservation. Hence the sojourn of Indians in this State will be sure to lead to strife, contention, and war, besides entailing an enormous expense to feed and provide for them. Again, there is no hope of civilizing these Indians while they reside in Colorado, as all the arable land in the State is required for its white settlers. A mining population needs in its immediate vicinity abundant facilities for agriculture to feed it. The question of feeding the white population of the State is one of paramount importance, and will certainly force itself on the attention of the government.[11]

The maps showing the loss of Indian lands in Colorado are a testament to the state's ethnic cleansing of Indians.[12]

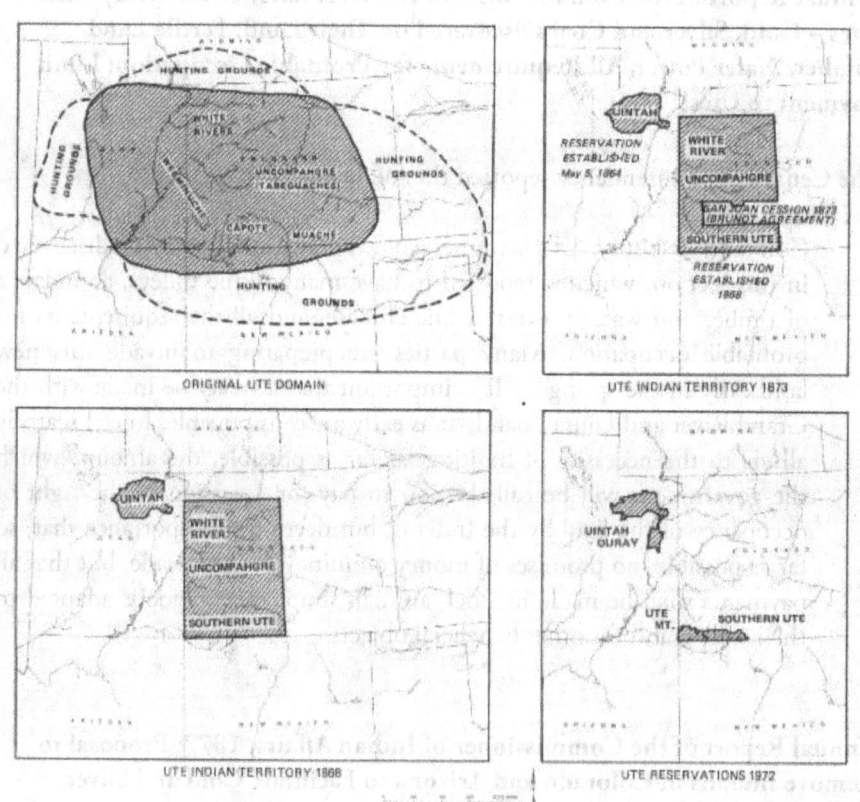

Relocation Program Effect on Colorado

In 1948, the BIA launched an off-reservation job-placement program for Navajos and Hopis. Placement offices were located in Denver, Los Angeles and Salt Lake City. More than 90 percent of the jobs offered to the Navajos and Hopis were seasonal, primarily in railroad construction or agriculture.

The relocation program ameliorated conservative criticism analogizing Indian communal living to socialism. In 1953, Senator George Malone of Montana gave voice to this position:

> While we are spending billions of dollars fighting communism and Marxist socialism throughout the world, we are at the same time, through the Indian Bureau, perpetuating the systems of Indian reservations and tribal government, which are natural Socialist environments.[13]

The relocation program, like Indian education at off-reservation boarding schools, attempted to enhance assimilation among the Indian people by placing them into white urban communities and ending the connection between American Indians and their traditional culture. BIA officers stressed the importance of detachment of the relocatees from their reservation communities from the program's outset. Its Manual for Counseling, presented in 1957, at the Gallup Area Conference of the BIA's Branch of Relocation Services emphasized discouraging commuting between the city and reservation.[14]

In 1953, Commissioner Dillon S. Myer justified relocation as the "liberation" of the American Indian population from "something akin to large detention camps."[15]

In 1950, the BIA extended its relocation program to other tribes, choosing Denver for its headquarters, as Denver was a popular destination for relocatees. A brochure, with enlarged letters saying "Come to Denver: The Chance of Your Lifetime!," showed pictures of a smiling family, a young Indian studying at school, a middle-aged Indian on a forklift truck, and a beautiful mountain in Colorado. It suggested that if relocatees would come to Denver, they could obtain "Good Jobs, Happy Homes, Training," and enjoy "Beautiful Colorado."

Realizing the problems faced by relocatees, the Commission on Community Relations of the City and County of Denver formed the Committee for Study of Relocated Indians on October 30, 1957, "to ascertain whether or not the program of the Relocation Service of the United States Bureau of Indian Affairs was placing an undue burden on City agencies. On April 2, 1958, the Denver Commission on Human Relations submitted to Mayor Nicholson a report entitled, "Indians in Denver-Relocated and NonRelocated." The report revealed that many relocatees suffered from severe poverty.[16]

By the early-1970s, however, as Indian policy strongly emphasized Indian self-determination and economic development on reservations, the relocation program disappeared. In 1973 Commissioner, Bureau of Indian Affairs, Louis R. Bruce explained the redirection of the relocation and employment assistance program as follows:

> The Bureau of Indian Affairs employment assistance program will redirect its present operation, directed toward moving Indians off reservation to cities, to one of developing manpower on reservations to complement economic development on the reservations. More employment assistance resources will be spent in reservation communities, thereby adding fuel to the reservation economies.

Many American Indians relocated to Denver stayed in Denver. Rather than assimilate into the white environment, they formed a new identity as 'urban' Indians and created pan-Indian organizations such as the White Buffalo Council and the Denver Indian Center.

NOTES:

1. Report of the Commissioner of Indian Affairs to the Secretary of the Interior, United States. Office of Indian Affairs, U.S. Government Printing Office, 1889.

2. Report of the Commissioner of Indian Affairs to the Secretary of the Interior, United States. Office of Indian Affairs, U.S. Government Printing Office, 1859.

3. Report of the Commissioner of Indian Affairs to the Secretary of the Interior, United States. Office of Indian Affairs, U.S. Government Printing Office, 1856.

4. Report of the Commissioner of Indian Affairs to the Secretary of the Interior, United States. Office of Indian Affairs, U.S. Government Printing Office, 1859.

5. Report of the Commissioner of Indian Affairs to the Secretary of the Interior, United States. Office of Indian Affairs, U.S. Government Printing Office, 1860.

6. Report of the Commissioner of Indian Affairs to the Secretary of the Interior, United States. Office of Indian Affairs, U.S. Government Printing Office, 1863.

7. Report of the Commissioner of Indian Affairs to the Secretary of the Interior, United States. Office of Indian Affairs, U.S. Government Printing Office, 1864.

8. Report of the Commissioner of Indian Affairs to the Secretary of the Interior, United States. Office of Indian Affairs, U.S. Government Printing Office, 1865.

9. Report of the Commissioner of Indian Affairs to the Secretary of the Interior, United States. Office of Indian Affairs, U.S. Government Printing Office, 1866.

10. Report of the Commissioner of Indian Affairs to the Secretary of the Interior, United States. Office of Indian Affairs, U.S. Government Printing Office, 1867.

11. Report of the Commissioner of Indian Affairs to the Secretary of the Interior, United States. Office of Indian Affairs, U.S. Government Printing Office, 1878.

12. https://www.irunfar.com/a-totally-serious-history-of-silverton-colorado (accessed online August 8, 2021).

13. http://nativeamericannetroots.net/diary/1356 (accessed online August 8, 2021).

14. https://kuscholarworks.ku.edu/bitstream/handle/1808/5808/ins.v05.n1.27-50.pdf?sequence=1 (accessed online April 8, 2021).

15. Ibid.

16. Ibid.

PART 26 / American Indian Education

2021 Federal Indian Boarding School Initiative

On June 22, 2021, Secretary of Interior Haaland directed the Department of Interior to prepare a report regarding the federal Indian boarding school program. The recent discovery of 215 unmarked graves by Canada's Tk'emlúps te Secwepemc First Nation at the Kamloops Indian Residential School prompted the Department of Interior to undertake this new initiative with the goal of shedding light on these past traumas. Also, at another site in Canada, around 700 unmarked graves at a boarding school site were discovered.

The 2021 Press Release stated in part as follows:

> The Federal Indian Boarding School Initiative will serve as an investigation about the loss of human life and the lasting consequences of residential Indian boarding schools. The primary goal will be to identify boarding school facilities and sites; the location of known and possible student burial sites located at or near school facilities; and the identities and Tribal affiliations of children interred at such locations.[1]

Conversion to Christianity and Education Seen as Solution

President Ulysses S. Grant under his Peace Policy announced on December 4, 1871, focused on assimilating the Indians and transforming them from "savages" into "civilized" men. The federal government gave money directly to Catholic and Protestant churches to convert Indians to Christianity and provide a white education to Indian children. Boarding schools were constructed and teachers hired.

At the same time of this Peace Policy and Christian focus, the Commissioner of Indian Affairs, A. B. Greenwood, reported to the Secretary of the Interior in November 1872, that it was "providential mercy" that the Indians were being rapidly overcome and they would have to yield to the white settlement of their land or perish.²

Annual Report of the Commissioner of Indian Affairs, 1877: Kill the Indian in Him and Save the Man

Commissioner of Indian Affairs E. A. Hayt expressed his position on Indian education to the Secretary of the Interior in 1877, as follows:

> Undoubtedly our chief hope is in the education of the young... I would advise the establishment of a rule making it compulsory upon all Indian children between the ages of six and fourteen years to attend schools, and requiring English alone to be spoken and taught therein; and it is decidedly preferable that as many of them as possible should be placed in boarding-schools, which possess more advantages in every way than day-schools, for the reason that the exposure of children who attend only day-schools to the demoralization and degradation of an Indian home neutralizes the efforts of the schoolteacher ...³

In a speech in 1892, The Advantages of Mingling Indians with Whites, Captain Pratt said:

> In his oft-referenced 1892 speech, Pratt stated, "A great general has said that the only good Indian is a dead one, and that high sanction of his destruction has been an enormous factor in promoting Indian massacres. In a sense, I agree with the sentiment, but only in this: that all the Indian there is in the race should be dead. Kill the Indian in him, and save the man."⁴

> Also, "In Indian civilization I am a Baptist," Pratt wrote, "because I believe in immersing the Indians in our civilization and when we get them under holding them there until they are thoroughly soaked."⁵

Richard Henry Pratt, founder of the Carlisle Indian Boarding School in Pennsylvania, which was operated from 1879-1918, explained the purpose of taking Indians to boarding schools to Spotted Tail of the Sioux Nation:

> There is no more chance for your people to keep themselves away from the whites. You are compelled to meet them. Your children will have to live with them. They will be all about and among you in spite of anything you can do, or that can be done for you by those interested in keeping you apart from our people. Your own welfare while you live and the welfare of your children after you, and all your interests in every way, demand that your children should have the same education that the white man has, that they should speak his language and know just how the white man lives, be able to meet him face to face without the help of either an interpreter or an Indian agent.[6]

In 1978 in *The Indian Student Amid American Inconsistencies*, Vine Deloria, Jr., with incredible clarity, elucidates on Indian education:

> Indian Education has been built upon the premise that the Indian had a great deal to learn from the white man; the white man representing the highest level of achievement reached in the evolutionary process The white man's religion was the best, his economics superior, his sense of justice the keenest, his knowledge of history the greatest. The Indian's task was to consume bits and pieces of the white man's world in the expectation that some day he would become as smart. The totality of the white man's knowledge was supposed to encompass the wisdom of the ages, painfully accumulated by a series of brilliant men.[7]

While the curriculum at Carlisle Indian School of Pennsylvania was vocational and academic, by 1898, under Superintendent of Indian Education Estelle Read, it would be primarily vocational.

Annual Report of the Commissioner of Indian Affairs, 1887: Progress toward Civilization includes Education

In 1887, Commissioner J. D. C. Adkins in his Annual Report to the Secretary, proclaimed his "three tests of progress toward civilization, viz, the adoption of the dress of the white man, engaging in agriculture, and the education of their children."[8]

The BIA's practice of counting how many members of a particular tribe wore the clothing of whites was meticulously detailed in Annual Indian Agent Reports. As early as 1858, Commissioner Charles E. Fix's Annual Report describes celebrating this change of dress:

They are rapidly putting aside their barbaric costume and ornaments, and adopting the dress, as well as the habits and pursuits, of civilized life. The plan devised by the superintendent and agent of having them signify their determination to do this in an open and formal manner, by being shorn of their scalp-locks-the peculiar and distinctive badge of the savage warrior- and assuming the dress of the white man, is well calculated not only to confirm the transformation in those making the change, but also to have a powerful effect and influence upon their brethren to follow their example.[9]

Annual Report of the Commissioner of Indian Affairs, 1894: Education to Convert Indians into American Citizens; Education Should Seek Disintegration of Tribes; Inculcate U.S. Patriotism; Indians to Attend Public Schools[10]

With regard to his philosophy of Indian education, Commissioner Morgan wrote:

When we speak of the education of the Indians we mean the comprehensive training and instruction which will convert them into American citizens, put within their reach the blessings which the rest of us enjoy, and enable them to compete successfully with the white man on his own ground and with his own methods. Education is to be the medium through which the rising generation of Indians are to be brought into the fraternal and harmonious relationship with their white fellow-citizens and with them enjoy the sweets of refined homes, the delight of social intercourse, the emoluments of commerce and trade, the advantages of travel, together with the pleasures that come from literature, science, and philosophy, and the solace and stimulus afforded by a true religion

With regard to education, Morgan felt that Indian history should not be taught and that it was important that Indian children acquire a fervent patriotism for the United States. In stressing patriotism, he ordered that all Indian schools celebrate national holidays: Washington's birthday, Decoration Day, the Fourth of July, Thanksgiving, and Christmas. Furthermore, he ordered that the American flag be displayed and that the students be taught reverence for the flag as a symbol of American protection and power.

According to the Commissioner: "Education should seek the disintegration of the tribes, and not their segregation. They should be educated, not as Indians, but as Americans."

In 1894, Commissioner T. J. Morgan proposed to place as many Indian children as possible in public schools.

Annual Report of the Commissioner of Indian Affairs, 1899: Education Turned from Tepee, Chase and Barbaric Savage Life to Civilization

In language repeatedly and consistently demeaning Indians, Commissioner W. A. Jones' 1899 Annual Report describes the education system and the knowledge transmitted:

> The educational system is therefore a broad and comprehensive one, and includes not only that which is taught the white boy and girl in our public schools, but also that which they learn at the fireside and in Christian homes. Their thoughts are turned from the tepee, the chase, and the barbaric ease of a savage life, when they would
>
> Wallow naked in December snow
>
> By thinking on fantastic summer's heat.

His Report continues:

> This policy, by force of circumstances, is based upon the well-known inferiority of the great mass of Indians in religion, intelligence, morals, and home life.
>
> The hope of the Indian race lies in taking the child at the tender age of four or five years, before the trend of his mind has become fixed in ancient molds or bent by the whims of his parents, and guiding it into the proper channel.
>
> Special attention is paid in the Government schools to the inculcation of patriotism. The Indian pupils are taught that they are Americans, that the Government is their friend, that the flag is their flag, that the one great duty resting on them is loyalty to the Government, and thus the foundation is laid for perpetual peace between the Indian tribes in this country and the white people.[11]

Annual Report of the Commissioner of Indian Affairs, 1901: Get Students by Cajolery, Threats, Bribery, Fraud, Persuasion or Force

In his 1901 Annual Report, Commissioner W. A. Jones reveals his distaste for the education program. His spite-filled analysis is quoted in full:

> There are in operation at the present time 113 boarding schools, with an average attendance of something over 16,000 pupils, ranging from 5 to 21 years old. These pupils are gathered from the cabin, the wickiup, and the tepee. Partly by cajolery and partly by threats; partly by bribery and partly by fraud; partly by persuasion and partly by force, they are induced to leave their homes and their kindred to enter these schools and take upon themselves the outward semblance of civilized life. They are chosen not on account of any particular merit of their own, not by reason of mental fitness, but solely because they have Indian blood in their veins. Without regard to their worldly condition; without any previous training; without any preparation whatever, they are transported to the schools-sometimes thousands of miles away-without the slightest expense or trouble to themselves or their people.
>
> The Indian youth finds himself at once, as if by magic, translated from a state of poverty to one of affluence. He is well fed and clothed and lodged. Books and all the accessories of learning are given him and teachers provided to instruct him. He is educated in the industrial arts on the one hand, and not only in the rudiments but in the liberal arts on the other. Beyond "the three r's" he is instructed in geography, grammar, and history; he is taught drawing, algebra and geometry, music, and astronomy, and receives lessons in physiology, botany, and entomology. Matrons wait on him while he is well and physicians and nurses attend him when he is sick. A steam laundry does his washing and the latest modern appliances do his cooking. A library affords him relaxation for his leisure hours, athletic sports and the gymnasium furnish him exercise and recreation, while music entertains him in the evening. He has hot and cold baths, and steam heat and electric light, and all the modern conveniences. All of the necessities of life are given him and many of the luxuries. All of this without money and without price, or the contribution of a single effort of his own or of his people. His wants are all supplied almost for the wish. The child of the wigwam becomes a modern Aladdin, who has only to rub the Government lamp to gratify his desires.
>
> Here he remains until his education is finished, when he is returned to his

home-which by contrast must seem squalid indeed-to the parents whom his education must make it difficult to honor, and left to make his way against the ignorance and bigotry of his tribe. Is it any wonder he fails? Is it surprising if he lapses into barbarism? Not having earned his education, it is not appreciated; having made no sacrifice to obtain it, it is not valued. It is looked upon as a right and not as a privilege; it is accepted as a favor to the Government and not to the recipient, and the almost inevitable tendency is to encourage dependence ...[12]

For an Indian view of the boarding school experience see In the White Man's Image, PBS video, and Healing the Hurts, another video.

Meriam Report, 1928, Boarding Schools Inadequate

A scientific study of American Indians was authorized by the Department of the Interior in 1926. Lewis Meriam led the study for the Institute for Government Research, a privately endowed foundation.

In 1928, the Meriam Report—The Problem of Indian Administration—was completed. The study contained data on health, education, economic development, social life, and government programs. Historian Kathleen Chamberlain, in her book *Under Sacred Ground: A History of Navajo Oil 1922-1982*, writes: "The Meriam Report captured the attention of government officials with graphic descriptions of poverty, disease, inadequate diet, and substandard housing."

The report is particularly critical of the boarding schools:

> "The survey staff finds itself obligated to say frankly and unequivocally that the provisions for the care of the Indian children in boarding schools are grossly inadequate."

While Indian education has often assumed that Indians are to be trained for manual labor, the report states:

> "The Indian Service should encourage promising Indian youths to continue their education beyond the boarding schools and to fit themselves for professional, scientific, and technical callings. Not only should the educational facilities of the boarding schools provide definitely for fitting them for college entrance, but the Service should aid them in meeting the costs."[13]

NOTES:

1. https://www.doi.gov/pressreleases/secretary-haaland-announces-federal-indian-boarding-school-initiative (accessed online August 8, 2021).

2. Report of the Commissioner of Indian Affairs to the Secretary of the Interior, United States. Office of Indian Affairs, U.S. Government Printing Office, 1873.

3. Report of the Commissioner of Indian Affairs to the Secretary of the Interior, United States. Office of Indian Affairs, U.S. Government Printing Office, 1878.

4. https://upstanderproject.org/firstlight/pratt (accessed online April 8, 2021).

5. Ibid.

6. Weinberg, Marjorie. *The real Rosebud: The triumph of a Lakota woman.* U of Nebraska Press, 2004.

7. Vine Deloria, Jr., "The Indian Student Amid American Inconsistencies," The Schooling of Native America, Thomas Thompson, ed. (Washington D.C.: American Association of Colleges for Teacher Education, 1978), 25.

8. Report of the Commissioner of Indian Affairs to the Secretary of the Interior, United States. Office of Indian Affairs, U.S. Government Printing Office, 1888.

9. Report of the Commissioner of Indian Affairs to the Secretary of the Interior, United States. Office of Indian Affairs, U.S. Government Printing Office, 1859.

10. Report of the Commissioner of Indian Affairs to the Secretary of the Interior, United States. Office of Indian Affairs, U.S. Government Printing Office, 1895.

11. Report of the Commissioner of Indian Affairs to the Secretary of the Interior, United States. Office of Indian Affairs, U.S. Government Printing Office, 1900.

12. Report of the Commissioner of Indian Affairs to the Secretary of the Interior, United States. Office of Indian Affairs, U.S. Government Printing Office, 1902.

13. Lewis Meriam, The Problems of Indian Administration (Baltimore: The Johns Hopkins Press, 1928).

PART 27 / Conclusion - No Satisfactory Completion of Civil Government Course Required to Graduate, Including History, Culture and Social Contributions of American Indians

Native News Online Article, August 27, 2021[1] - No Comment by Governor; CO DOE – We Don't Audit for Compliance; CCSD - "While Indigenous History Is Definitely Taught In Numerous High School Social Studies Courses, *"I Cannot Speak To The Consistency And Depth In Each Relevant Course."*

In an article by Jenna Kunze, *Native News Online* reporter, the governor's office declined to comment.

A "spokesperson for the Cherry Creek School District, Abbe Smith, told *Native News Online* that "while Indigenous history is definitely taught in numerous high school social studies courses, *I cannot speak to the consistency and depth in each relevant course."* …

According to a Colorado Department of Education spokesperson, Joanne Bruno, *there is no audit of schools' compliance*. "The mechanism we have in place is we have a state assessment in social studies," she said. "That's one way to develop accountability in what's in our standards. Outside of that, there is no specific mechanism." Bruno said she was unaware of Harvey's petition but has "no reasons to believe" that schools are out of compliance with the law. "Indigenous Peoples history is part of US and CO history, which are part of our state standards," she said. …

At the Southern Ute Indian Tribe —one of two federally recognized tribes in the state—Director of Education LaTitia Taylor told Native News Online that the materials are there, it's just *a matter of building relationships with school districts to implement them.* She worked with the state to develop a 4th grade curriculum on the Ute people of Colorado. (Emphasis added).

Pall of Orthodoxy v. Academic Freedom

In *State Bd. for Community Colleges v. Olson*, 687 P.2d 429, 437 (Colo. 1984) (quoting *Keyishian v. Board of Regents*, 385 U.S. 589, 606 (1967)), the Colorado Appellate Court expresses the following regarding academic freedom:

> Our Nation is deeply committed to safeguarding academic freedom, which is of transcendent value to all of us and not merely to the teachers concerned. That freedom is therefore a special concern of the First Amendment, which does not tolerate laws that cast a pall of orthodoxy over the classroom. The vigilant protection of constitutional freedoms is nowhere more vital than in the community of American schools. *Shelton v. Tucker*, 364 U.S. 479, 487 [(1960)]. The classroom is peculiarly the 'marketplace of ideas.' The Nation's future depends on leaders trained through wide exposure to that robust exchange of ideas which discovers truth 'out of a multitude of tongues [rather] than through any kind of authoritative selection.' *United States v. Associated Press*, 52 F. Supp. 362, 372 [(S.D.N.Y. 1943)].

Obligatory Status of § 22-1-104 - Satisfactory Completion of Civil Government Course Required to Graduate, Including History, Culture and Social Contributions of American Indians

The obligatory status of § 22-1-104 has been confirmed by the Colorado state legislature, the Colorado Governor, the CO DOE, the Colorado Attorney General and the federal and state judiciary; school districts boards of education such as the CCSD BOE; school district administrations such as Jeffco, the PSD and the CCSD. It has been endorsed by the CO EA and numerous school districts have adopted it as part of their Graduation Requirements in adopting the CASB Policy on Graduation Requirements ("CASB IKF"), recommended by the CO DOE. Students have a right to receive mandated instruction and to be assured that their diploma is valid. The U.S. Supreme Court has ruled that students have a protected property interest in a high school diploma. The implementation of § 22-1-104(1) is long overdue.

Action Required to Ensure Compliance with § 22-1-104 - Satisfactory Completion of Civil Government Course in Order to Graduate, Including History, Culture and Social Contributions of American Indians

It is imperative that the CCSD BOE self-report to the CO DOE that it does not have a § 22-1-104 course, if it does not, not just a HB 19-1192 course. If it does not, it would appear it is not in compliance with state law as assured under its contract on file with the CO DOE. There is no reason for Colorado school districts to not have been in compliance with § 22-1-104 starting in 2007.

The Governor, the Attorney General and the CO DOE absolutely must initiate and investigate immediately across the state to determine what school districts, if any, are not in compliance with § 22-1-104. From 2007 forward, the state's public and charter schools high school diplomas may be tainted with an alleged complicity and misrepresentation of state public school administrators and staff certifying individual students as qualified to receive a Colorado state high school diploma, when the public school may not have been in non-compliance with § 22-1-104. The validity of these diplomas is subject to judicial attack if false certifications have been made to the public. This investigation must include accreditation under the assurance contracts filed by each Colorado school district with the CO DOE certifying their compliance with federal and state laws.

The CO DOE must investigate which federal funding applications it has submitted included a representation that such a § 22-1-104 course is required, subjecting the state to a claim of false representation to the federal government. These should be promptly corrected. A nationwide statement must be issued if the alleged compliance is factual, so that websites may correct any misrepresentative information to the public.

All Colorado high school public and charter parents and students must be clearly informed of their rights under § 22-1-104 through a vast media notice to assure they have this requisite information. This is a statewide and national imperative, as former Colorado high school graduates may have moved out of state, and high school students may be moving to Colorado without this information.

There is enforceability in requiring compliance with § 22-1-104 and that is through OUR state government (executive, legislative, administrative and judicial bodies) and public action. Colorado Revised Statute § 22-1-104 does have "teeth."

There are those, though, who use specious arguments allowing for the unlawful ethnic cleansing of minorities from the Colorado high school education arena. Peter d'Errico characterized this so artfully as a "semantic world created by one group to rule another."[2]

Federal Government Assistance Needed in Colorado - (1) Enforcement of § 22-1-104 which May Be Ignored based on Minority Protected Classes Intended to Benefit from § 22-1-104, Violating Constitutional Rights to Life, Liberty and Property (e.g., Valid Diploma); (2) Investigation of CCSD's Institutional Racism's Impact on CCSD "Consistent, Pervasive and Predictable" Minority Academic Achievement Gap; and (3) Investigation of CCSD's Institutional Racism's Impact on Discipline Statistics for Minorities which Continue to Demonstrate Pattern of Disparate Impact, Including American Indians, Notwithstanding CCSD-OCR Resolution Agreement of 2018

The United States Department of Justice ("US DOJ") and the United States Office of Civil Rights ("U.S. OCR) fulfill their mission to protect civil rights in many ways, including by (1) responding to civil rights complaints filed by members of the public; (2) proactively conducting compliance reviews and directed investigations to enforce Federal civil rights laws; (3) monitoring recipients' adherence to resolution agreements; (4) issuing policy guidance to increase recipients' understanding of their civil rights obligations and students' and families' awareness of students' civil rights; (5) providing technical assistance and other information to recipients and the public; and (6) administering and disseminating civil rights information.

The federal government must take action just as it did in Little Rock, Arkansas, in 1957, due to white resistance to school desegregation resulting in open defiance of the law and violent confrontations. With the militia presence at the CCSD BOE meetings, and subsequently the heavy armed guard presence for the public's protection, the possibility of violent confrontations is not out of the question. All that is needed at this point is (1) the enforcement of an eighteen-year-old legislatively mandate requiring high school students to satisfactorily complete one-half semester course of civil government, **including**, not solely on, the history, culture and social contributions of certain minorities; (2) an investigation of CCSD's institutional racism's impact on the CCSD "consistent, pervasive and predictable" Minority Academic Achievement Gap; and (3) an investigation of CCSD's institutional racism's impact on the Discipline Statistics for Minorities Which Continue to Demonstrate a Pattern of Disparate Impact, including American Indians, notwithstanding the CCSD-OCR Resolution Agreement of 2018. Parents deserve to know if their children are being unfairly graded, failing, possibly held-back a grade, assigned to Special Education classes, encouraged to transfer to another school district, or more harshly disciplined in comparison to Anglo students. They may have blamed their children for something beyond their control.

Anarchy in Colorado's Public School System

If a commander can't get a soldier to polish his boots, how does he get him to engage in battle.

If drivers don't have to stop for red lights because there are no consequences, we have chaos—property damage and personal injury and death.

If a school does not have to teach an eighteen-year-old legislatively mandated one half semester course of civil government, including, not solely on, the history, culture and social contributions of certain minorities, we have anarchy in the school system.

The Colorado legislature can't get the school districts to teach the course.

The Colorado governor can't get the school districts to teach the course.

The Colorado judiciary can't get the school districts to teach the course.

The Colorado Department of Education can't get the school districts to teach the course.

The Cherry Creek School District Board of Education can't get the school district to teach the course.

Any person engaged in certifying students for graduation who have not taken and satisfactorily completed the 22-1-104 course are being forced to misrepresent the students' status. If this is occurring, it is gross negligence, if not fraud, on the part of the Superintendent and Board.

Any school personnel using federal funds, while not complying with the requirements, are engaged in duplicitous behavior.

The state is out of control. Students' civil rights are being trampled on.

NOTES:

1. *Native News Online* Article, August 27, 2021

2. d'Errico, Peter. "American Indian sovereignty: Now you see it, now you don't." *Decolonising Indigenous Rights*. Routledge, 2008. 115-131. https://people.umass.edu/derrico/nowyouseeit.html (accessed online November 4, 2020).

PART 28 / Post-Script - No Satisfactory Completion of Civil Government Course Required to Graduate, Including History, Culture and Social Contributions of American Indians; Minority Achievement Gap, Including American Indians; Disparate Discipline of Minorities, Including American Indians

Native American Holocaust Honor Song

    We survived or we died.
    In battle, in massacres, in prisoner-of-war camps, in forced marches, in cruel removal, in boarding schools, in re-location to cities, in termination of our tribes, in jails, in shame and despair, our deities mocked.

    We survived or we died.
    We survived or we died, our heroism forgotten.
    In lives shattered by colonialism,
    Stifled by oppression,
    Shamed by assimilation,
    Silenced by subjection,
    We survived or we died.

    We survived or we died, our valor overlooked.
    In lives filled with hatred,
    Bigotry,
    Apathy,
    Oblivion,
    We survived or we died.

    We survived or we died, our courage dismissed.

Unable to mourn the loss of lives,
Land and resources,
Culture,
Our continuing genocide.
We survived or we died.

We survived or we died, our strength ignored.
We are voices out of the darkness.
We are voices of honor.
We are voices of truth.
We are voices of life.
We are voices of hope.

Hear our pain.
Hear our suffering.
Hear our anguish.
Hear our despair.

In a perpetual state of grief,
We survived or we died.

Native American Holocaust in Colorado's Public High Schools

We survived or we died
In Colorado's public high schools -
Unable to get the school system to add one course
Only including, not wholly about, our history, culture and social contributions
Education paramount for the privileged Anglos.

We failed to achieve, we failed to graduate
We dropped out, we drugged ourselves into a stupor to escape
We hated ourselves for being Indian or we assimilated into the Majority
Unable to endure the ignominy of being different, of being less than.

We survived or we died
Harshly, disproportionately disciplined
Captive this time in public schools
Alone, with no one to help.

We survived or we died
Colorado's public high schools flaunting the law in our face
Enduring its continuing, unabated, injustices
Its quiet massacres.

Addendum

Colorado Students Aren't Supposed To Graduate Without Learning About Indigenous History And Culture Are They? By Jenny Brundin, September 30, 2021, Colorado Public Radio News (https://www.cpr.org/2021/09/30/colorado-students-arent-supposed-to-graduate-without-learning-about-indigenous-history-and-culture-are-they/) (Accessed online October 1, 2021).

Navajo Carol Harvey walks back and forth outside the State Capitol several days a week to bring awareness to what she alleges is a lack of Indigenous content in school curriculum as Colorado law requires. She recalls her ancestors who were forcibly marched 400 miles from their homeland. "This march of mine is a moral act ... it's a sacred commitment on my part."

You may have seen her.

She's a lone Indigenous woman, fanny pack filled with water, walking sticks at her sides, striding back and forth along the same Downtown Denver block. She strides in front of the state Capitol, hoping Governor Jared Polis notices her and a petition she's sent him.

"This march of mine is a moral act ... it's a sacred commitment on my part," said Carol Harvey, 70.

She said 160 years ago the U.S. government forcibly marched Navajos 400 miles away from their homeland to parts of Arizona and New Mexico. Starvation, slavery, prostitution, and disease followed.

"If I can't walk a few miles here until this course is satisfied ... well, I'm willing to go 600 miles," said Harvey, who wore a T-shirt that says "Enforce 22-1-104."

The "course" Harvey is talking about is Colorado's only state high school graduation requirement, referred to in statute 22-1-104. State lawmakers mandated that American Indians be included in Colorado curriculum in 1998. They widened that in 2004, and this became the graduation requirement: Students must take a civil government course which includes the history, culture and social contributions of African Americans, Latinos, and Indigenous people. The law was further amended in 2019 to include other groups, too.

But some say tens of thousands of students graduate each year in the state without learning what's mandated in that single state graduation requirement. They graduate anyway—and some people say no one seems to care.

Harvey, a former attorney, said the Cherry Creek School District, where her grandchildren go to school, doesn't offer a civil government course that deals with those areas despite the fact that Colorado judges have upheld the law three times.

"My concern is—[the] civil rights are being violated of these students," she said.

A Cherry Creek school district official said in a June school board meeting that the district is in compliance with the law.

The story is the same around the state.

Now this gets nuanced. School districts like Cherry Creek say they do teach Indigenous content—a couple of the district's high schools offer an "ethnic studies" course. But—those classes are electives, aren't taught in every school and are not mandatory. Some Indigenous content may also turn up in history classes, for instance, not in a government course like the law specifies. Indigenous references, for example, may crop up during a history lesson on Manifest Destiny or westward expansion, where teachers might discuss treaties or assimilation.

"So, then we'll pop up in a paragraph or a few sentences .... But there's never enough content to really give perspective," said Donna Chrisjohn, a mother of five with several children in the Cherry Creek district, and a member of the Sicangu Lakota Nation and a descendant of the Diné Nation. She also teaches classes to teachers and administrators on Indigenous history and culture for a perspective they don't necessarily know or understand.

Donna Chrisjohn, a mother of five with several children in the Cherry Creek district, sits with her daughter Tanksi, 11. She wants all children to have access to Indigenous content in schools.

'Our invisibility and our erasure in this country is on purpose'

Christjohn said some individual teachers in Colorado make real efforts to include Indigenous content, often in a history or English class. One Denver teacher begins her history course having students read selections from An Indigenous Peoples' History of the United States. But advocates say the content of most government courses, such as civics classes, far from satisfies what Colorado law specifies students be taught.

Instead, Chrisjohn said, curriculum is often rife with generalizations, romanticization and stereotypes. Modern day Indigenous issues are almost never discussed. Also often ignored is the fact that Indigenous people existed in America up to 20,000 years prior to 1492.

"There's actually no context to the fact we existed here prior to settler colonialism," Chrisjohn said. "Our invisibility and our erasure in this country is on purpose. It is built in through federal policies and it is institutionalized in our school systems."

She said a civics class could include Indigenous ways of governing, handling conflict, Indigenous values systems, the theory that U.S. democracy was influenced by the 6 Nations of the Iroquois Confederacy, federal policy and jurisdictional issues, and sovereignty rights.

She said teachers don't have to start from scratch. Montana, Washington, Minnesota, Nebraska, and South and North Dakota have well-developed curriculum that teachers could draw from initially.

"I think the civics course is necessary to have a true understanding of this country, who we are, and the things that we have done in our past and how laws came to be," she said. "And we're not learning that."

The state sets academic standards, but local districts choose how to teach it.

The Colorado Department of Education's Joanna Bruno confirmed that Colorado students do indeed have to take a government/civics course that includes "the history, culture and social contributions of minorities" including Indigenous people.

"Examples of social contributions could be the different ways that different cultures contributed to our government or to our society at the U.S. level or Colorado level," said Bruno, the director of the state's office of standards and instructional support.

In Colorado, the state sets the academic standards. But it's local districts that choose the curriculum they want to use to meet those standards. Bruno said districts in the Four Corners area, for example, may have more Indigenous content than districts in northeast Colorado.

"The intention of local control is to allow communities flexibility in that implementation," Bruno said.

But has American Indian content, as the law has required since 1998, even been included in published state academic standards?

An analysis of the 2009 state social studies education standards found that, despite the law, the state didn't specify any concrete information that students must learn about living American Indians. In a teacher-authored sample curriculum published by state education officials in 2013, there are no references to American Indians, Black people or Latinos.

Donna Chrisjohn, a mother of five with children in the Cherry Creek school district, is an education consultant and has been presenting the Indigenous perspective to schools and organizations for 43 years.

A 2021analysis of the most recent Colorado social studies standards found that Native Americans appear in only two standards—once in fourth grade and once in sixth. In both cases Indigenous peoples are referred to in past context and "do not emphasize native sovereignty nor present day concerns of Indigenous peoples."

That report recommended state officials include Indigenous voices and representation to offer a more complete history and view of present-day thinking of Indigenous peoples.

As far as high school civics or history standards and whether they address Indigenous history, culture and social contributions, Harvey noted that the word "tribal" is simply inserted every time there is a reference to "local, state, and national" in civics standards. That's it.

Bruno said there's no audit of Colorado schools' compliance with the law when it comes to learning about Indigenous people. But, she said she thinks schools are likely teaching what the law requires.

"I don't have any reason to believe that they aren't," she said. "Nothing's been brought to our attention about that."

Carol Harvey said she has sent a petition calling for an audit to everyone imaginable – state education officials, the governor, the U.S. Department of Justice and the U.S. Office of Civil Rights.

Other states are fighting the 'erasure' of Indigenous content in schools. What's next for Colorado?

In South Dakota, more than a dozen references to an Indigenous tribe were stripped from new proposed social studies content. Montana brought together representatives from tribes to create an in-depth toolkit for teachers. Now, Montana is being sued for what some say is a failure to meet a constitutional mandate that guarantees every school teaches American Indian heritage in a culturally responsive way.

Some states like Wisconsin lay out specifically what Indigenous content should be taught and give examples from exemplar teachers, but a recent article explored how teachers say they don't know how to teach about Indigenous issues.

Could change be on the way in Colorado?

The state is in the midst of revising social studies standards to include more content about racial and ethnic minorities, as a result of legislation passed in 2019. That work should be finished by 2022 and must be implemented in the 2024-25 school year.

Meanwhile, Cherry Creek, along with other districts, are in the process of reviewing and choosing social studies curriculum as they wait for new state standards to come out.

"What we're constantly trying to do is to make sure the curricular resources that we use must reflect the students that are sitting in our classrooms," said Sarah Grobbel, an assistant superintendent with the Cherry Creek School District, at a June board meeting.

But other districts like Jefferson County, have already made changes to curriculum to reflect the requirements of the 2019 law.

Veteran high school social studies teacher Mark Sass said standards for what young people should learn in history and civics haven't changed much in a century. As far as what they should understand about the history of the United States, Sass said "there is nothing consistently across the state by which we could judge who's doing well with it and who's not."

"I think it's important for us to have a shared understanding of what we think these kids should know when they leave high school, especially with the conversations right now around diversity, equity and inclusion. These kids need to know about the role race plays in our country."

Navajo Carol Harvey, a former attorney, has sent a petition to state lawmakers, state education officials, and federal civil rights and justice officials asking for an audit of Colorado schools to determine if the history, culture and contributions of minorities, including Indigenous people is being taught in a civil government class as Colorado law specifies.

'Indigenous youth grow up learning that education spaces aren't for them.'

Donna Chrisjohn said in the Lakota belief system, children are a gift.

"We believe that they are our teachers. We learn from them. We get an opportunity to learn and grow. We honor them in our homes."

But the second a child enters school, it's the teacher who knows everything and children are expected to sit and listen in many classrooms.

"It's a totally different perspective. So how harmful is that for our Indigenous students to know that my culture, everything about myself can never come into this classroom because it will never be accepted?"

In a recent national report, the U.S. Commission on Civil Rights found that the lack of Indigenous representation in school curriculum harms students. It said without historically accurate representation or discussion of Native American people in curriculum, the education experience can be isolating and limiting. Donna Chrisjohn agrees.

"We know that right away, as soon as we start '1492 and sailing the ocean blue,' we know that that is not the truth of who we are and where we come from. And we are immediately erased," she said. "And then we're triggered that I'm just not included in this classroom perspective or this narrative."

Harvey said when you don't see yourself in the curriculum, when you don't see any positive examples of people who look like you, it's hard to feel engaged. The Native American graduation rate is nearly 67 percent in Colorado compared to 82 percent for all students statewide. A full 71 percent of Indigenous students don't meet reading and writing expectations. Eighty two percent of students aren't on grade level in math.

Typically, Indigenous people are portrayed in educational settings as a historic people who no longer have an active presence in civic life—87 percent of state history standards do not mention Native American history after 1900. State officials said recognizing Indigenous groups in the current and historical context is a recommendation from a commission created by the HB19-1192 law, which is recommending standards revisions.

Advocates for more Indigenous content would like to see that changed in order to reduce both racial stereotyping among all students and ignorance rooted in fear.

Carol Harvey and Donna Chrisjohn's ancestors have been here for 20,000 years. They say they're not going anywhere—and they're not giving up.

"It's time for school districts to act," Harvey said.

President Biden's Executive Order on the White House Initiative on Advancing Educational Equity, Excellence, and Economic Opportunity for Native Americans and Strengthening Tribal Colleges and Universities, Oct. 11, 2021

By the authority vested in me as President by the Constitution and the laws of the United States of America, it is hereby ordered as follows:

Section 1. Policy. The United States has a unique political and legal relationship with federally recognized Tribal Nations, as set forth in the Constitution of the United States, statutes, treaties, Executive Orders, and court decisions. The Federal Government is committed to protecting the rights and ensuring the well-being of Tribal Nations while respecting Tribal sovereignty and inherent rights of self-determination. In recognition of that commitment and to fulfill the solemn obligations it entails, executive departments and agencies (agencies) must help advance educational equity, excellence, and economic opportunity for Native American students, whether they attend public schools in urban, suburban, or rural communities; are homeschooled; attend primary and secondary schools operated or funded by the Bureau of Indian Education (BIE) of the Department of the Interior; or attend postsecondary educational institutions, including Tribal Colleges and Universities (TCUs).

For more than a century, the United States imposed educational policies designed to assimilate Native peoples into predominant United States culture that devastated Native American students and their families. Beginning with the Indian Civilization Act of 1819, the United States enacted laws and implemented policies establishing and supporting Indian boarding schools across the Nation. From 1871 onward, federally run Indian boarding schools were used to culturally assimilate Native American children who were forcibly removed from their families and communities and relocated to distant residential facilities where their Native identities, languages, traditions, and beliefs were forcibly suppressed. The conditions in these schools were usually harsh, and sometimes abusive and deadly. Although these policies have ended, their effects and resulting trauma reverberate in Native American communities even today, creating specific challenges that merit Federal attention and response.

The Federal Government must put strong focus on early childhood and K-12 educational opportunities. These are important to developing and strengthening Native American communities, and they set the stage for educational advancement and career development, including opportunities to attend TCUs.

It is the policy of my Administration to advance equity, excellence, and justice in our Nation's education system and to further Tribal self-governance, including by supporting activities that expand educational opportunities and improve educational outcomes for all Native American students. My Administration will help expand opportunities for Native American students to learn their Native languages, histories, and cultural practices; promote indigenous learning through the use of traditional ecological knowledge; and enhance access to complete and competitive educations that prepare Native American students for college, careers, and productive and satisfying lives.

(b) This order supersedes Executive Order 13592 of December 2, 2011 (Improving American Indian and Alaska Native Educational Opportunities and Strengthening Tribal Colleges and Universities), which is revoked. To the extent that there are other Executive Orders that may conflict with or overlap with the provisions in this order, the provisions in this order shall supersede those other Executive Orders on these subjects. (Emphasis added).

https://www.whitehouse.gov/briefing-room/presidential-actions/2021/10/11/executive-order-on-the-white-house-initiative-on-advancing-educational-equity-excellence-and-economic-opportunity-for-native-americans-and-strengthening-tribal-colleges-and-universities/

Non-Verbal Behavior of American Indian Students May Be Used against Them

The non-verbal behavior of American Indian students may be used against them. Administrators or faculty may think a student is being disrespectful or defiant when exhibiting certain non-verbal behaviors.

(1) Not looking them in the eye;
(2) Laughing or smiling (typical American Indian non-verbal behavior when scared)—it is a way to save face;
(3) Being silent;
(4) Fear of being singled out from a group causing nervous behavior;
(5) Walking with head down;
(6) Inability to explain or defend themselves; and
(7) Sense of defeat, fait acompli.

Certain of these behaviors have a legitimate purpose in American Indian society. For example, when living in close-quarters (as I did in a one-room home), it is considered polite to avert one's eyes and to look down when walking so as not to infringe upon the privacy of another. Silence is an honored behavior learned at an early age. The importance of tribal group identity makes it very frightening to be singled out. For many, even if they speak English, they do not have the ability to verbalize a defense. Most parents are afraid to come into a university setting, so they will leave it up to the student to go through the situation alone, unaided by an adult. Many parents feel that they do not have the understanding to confront administrators or an administrative process they do not understand. Many times the disruptive behavior is caused by the racism of others, and it is shaming to admit it.

Lack of Knowledge of Formal Register

Maria Rosario Montano-Harmon's outstanding research in this area is critical: She has found that "The hidden rules of the middle class govern schools and work; students from generational poverty come with a completely different set of hidden rules and do not know middle class hidden rules."

Hidden Rules

One key resource for success in school and at work is an understanding of the hidden rules. Hidden rules are the unspoken cueing system that individuals use to indicate membership in a group. One of the most important middle-class rules is that work and achievement tend to be the driving forces in decision-making. In generational poverty, the driving forces are survival, entertainment, and relationships. This is why a student may have a $30 Halloween costume but an unpaid book bill.

Formal register is standard business and educational language. Formal register is characterized by complete sentences and specific word choice.

Casual register is characterized by a 400 to 500 word vocabulary, broken sentences, and many non-verbal assists. Maria Montano-Harmon, a California researcher, has found that many low-income students know only casual register. Many discipline referrals occur because the student has spoken in casual register.

When individuals have no access to the structure and specificity of formal register, their achievement lags. This is complicated by the story structure used in casual register.

In formal register, the story structure focuses on plot, has a beginning and end, and weaves sequence, cause and effect, characters, and consequences into the plot.

In casual register, the focus of the story is characterization. Typically, the story starts at the end (Joey busted his nose), proceeds with short vignettes interspersed with participatory comments from the audience. (He hit him hard. BAMBAM. You shouda' seen the blood on him), and finishes with a comment about the character. (To see this in action, watch a TV talk show where many of the participants use this structure.) The story elements that are included are those with emotional significance for the teller. This is an episodic, random approach with many omissions. It does not include sequence, cause and effect, or consequences.

Physical fighting is how conflict is resolved. If you only know casual register, you don't have the words to negotiate a resolution. Respect is accorded to those who can physically defend themselves.

Reuven Feuerstein refers to these students as "unmediated." Simply explained mediation happens when an adult makes a deliberate intervention and does three things:

1. points out the stimulus (what needs to be paid attention to)
2. gives the stimulus meaning
3. provides a strategy to deal with the stimulus

For example: Don't cross the street without looking (stimulus). You could be killed (meaning). Look twice both ways before crossing (strategy).

Mediation builds cognitive strategies for the mind. The strategies are analogous to the infrastructure of a house, that is, the plumbing, electrical and heating systems. When cognitive strategies are only partially in place, the mind can only partially accept the teaching. According to Feuerstein, unmediated students may miss as much as 50 percent of text on a page.

Why are so many students unmediated? Poverty forces one's time to be spent on survival. Many students from poverty live in single parent families. When there is only one parent, she or he does not have time and energy to both mediate the children and work to put food on the table. And if the parent is non-mediated, her or his ability to mediate the children will be significantly lessened.1

Note

1. Understanding and Working with Students and Adults from Poverty, Ruby K. Payne, Ph.D., Founder and president of aha! Process, Inc., Extracted from BC Alternative Education Association Newsletter, Volume 15, Number 1, Spring 2004.

1890 – Colorado Not Happy With Southern Ute Indians Wants Them Gone Too. Report of the Commissioner of Indian Affairs to the Secretary of the Interior, United States. Office of Indian Affairs, U.S. Government Printing Office, 1891, p. XLIV.

The agreement made with the Southern Ute Indians, of Colorado, in the fall of 1888, which has excited great popular interest throughout the country, is still pending in Congress. Friends of the Indians are loth to believe that it will be for the best interests of the Indians to take them from the fertile valleys of their present reservation [IN CO] and settle them upon the barren, unproductive lands of the proposed reservation in Utah. ... This little band constitutes the last remnant of Indians in the great State of Colorado, and in comparison with the number of Indians in other States—South Dakota, Montana, Nebraska, California, etc.—is very small indeed. Removal merely shifts the burden of their presence from Colorado to Utah and delays their final civilization. As above stated, the Southern Utes are the only Indians now remaining in Colorado, and they number less than two thousand. Minnesota, Michigan, and Wisconsin each have over three times as many, Montana five, and California six times as many, North Dakota and South Dakota four and ten times as many, respectively, and the State of Washington five times as many; so that *in the distribution of our Indian population, to those who regard their presence as a detriment, Colorado seems to have been much more fortunate than many of her sister States.* (Emphasis added.)

COMMENTS CAROL HARVEY, RESIDENT CHERRY CREEK SCHOOL DISTRICT, COLORADO, COLORADO DEPARTMENT OF EDUCATION, Standards Review Committee – Social Studies

PART 1: Failed Social Studies Recommended Revisions

The Colorado Department of Education Standards Review Committee - Social Studies Recommended Revisions are a complete failure in responding to 22-1-104(2). The main problem is that they are based on a revision of the 2020 Colorado Academic Standards: Social Studies which were given the grade of "D" by the Thomas B. Fordham Institute, almost a complete failure in grading analysis. **A complete revision of the standards was recommended by the Fordham Institute.1**

Dr. Amber Northern, Senior Vice President for Research with The Thomas B. Fordham Institute interview with Ross Kaminsky on June 24, 2021, described Colorado's standards as "wishy-washy," "vague and amorphous." "The lack of detail is problematic." It's a "recipe for disaster" in holding students accountable. It's a "travesty" for the children of Colorado. Politically they aren't likely to offend anyone because they don't say anything. Colorado needs to "go back to the drawing board." (Emphasis added).2

YET THE CDE USED THESE FAILING STANDARDS AS THEIR BASIS FOR THEIR CURRENT 2021 DRAFT REVISION, MERELY ADDING A REFERENCE TO MINORITIES HERE AND THERE IN THE HISTORY STANDARDS, NOT THE CIVIC STANDARDS.

CO DOE Cites Mandatory Legislative § 22-1-104 Requirement Repeatedly on Its Public Website: Satisfactory Completion of Civil Government Course Required to Graduate, Including History, Culture and Social Contributions of American Indians

The CO DOE has consistently cited § 22-1-104 as a mandatory state law; its website has numerous specific references, including five as recently as February, July and August 2021.3

CO DOE – Graduation Guidelines – March 18, 2021

Note: Currently, Colorado's only statewide requirement for high school graduation is the satisfactory completion of a civics/government course that encompasses information on both the United States and State of Colorado (C.R.S. 22-1-104)

The only course required in state law for graduation is Civics (22-1-104 (3)(a) C.R.S). LEPs have the ability to determine how this course requirement is met.

The CO DOE used the same language in its CDE Graduation Guidelines (GG): Frequently Asked Questions – March 18, 2021, and August 4 and 11, 2021.

CO DOE Monitors School District Compliance with Graduation Guidelines Under an Honor System

The CO DOE monitors school districts compliance with its state Graduation Guidelines under accreditation contracts the school districts file with the CO DOE. The CO DOE is authorized to accredit schools.4

The school districts agree to "substantially comply with all statutory and regulatory requirements applicable to the District..." It is an honor system program as the CO DOE lacks the resources to audit school district compliance. There are consequences if the CO DOE determines that a school district is violating the state and regulatory requirements. First, the school district would have to be found to have violated the state and regulatory requirements which would require a CO DOE administrative procedure. If a violation is proven to have occurred, the school district will be allowed a time period to come into compliance. If it hasn't based on an administrative review, its accreditation could be impacted.5

As stated so eloquently by Donna Chrisjohn in an interview and article by Colorado Public Radio:

> **'Our invisibility and our erasure in this country is on purpose.'** Christjohn said some individual teachers in Colorado make real efforts to include Indigenous content, often in a history or English class. One Denver teacher begins her history course having students read selections from An Indigenous Peoples' History of the United States. But advocates say the content of most government courses, such as civics classes, far from satisfies what Colorado law specifies students be taught.
>
> Instead, Chrisjohn said, curriculum is often rife with generalizations, romanticization and stereotypes. Modern day Indigenous issues are almost never discussed. Also often ignored is the fact that Indigenous people existed in America up to 20,000 years prior to 1492.
>
> "There's actually no context to the fact we existed here prior to settler colonialism," Chrisjohn said. "Our invisibility and our erasure in this country is on purpose. It is built in through federal policies and it is institutionalized in our school systems."

She said a civics class could include Indigenous ways of governing, handling conflict, Indigenous values systems, the theory that U.S. democracy was influenced by the 6 Nations of the Iroquois Confederacy, federal policy and jurisdictional issues, and sovereignty rights.

She said teachers don't have to start from scratch. Montana, Washington, Minnesota, Nebraska, and South and North Dakota have well-developed curriculum that teachers could draw from initially.

"I think the civics course is necessary to have a true understanding of this country, who we are, and the things that we have done in our past and how laws came to be," she said. "And we're not learning that."6

The CDE Social Studies Recommended Revisions for Civics wholly ignore the legislative mandate of 22-1-104 to require the satisfactory completion of a civil government course for graduation, including the culture, history and social contributions of minorities. Colorado's illegal diplomas sanctioned by the CDE are tainted in the blood, sweat and tears of minority families who want a non-discriminatory education for their children.

A school superintendent in Arizona described his strategy against Mexican American studies by doing what "Hannibal did to the Romans, and when Hannibal encountered the Romans he stretched them out ... during which time the school district lost an enormous number of their Mexican–American students.7

I am afraid this is what Colorado is doing in failing to require the satisfactory completion of a civil government course for graduation, including the culture, history and social contributions of minorities.

As evidenced in the 1890 Commissioner of Indian Affairs Report to the Secretary of the Interior, Colorado wanted to remove the one remaining Indian tribe in Colorado, the Southern Utes. They did not succeed and the Commissioner of Indian Affairs noted Colorado should not be to overly concerned:

... the Southern Utes are the only Indians now remaining in Colorado, and they number less than two thousand. Minnesota, Michigan, and Wisconsin each have over three times as many, Montana five, and California six times as many, North Dakota and South Dakota four and ten times as many, respectively, and the State of Washington five times as many; so that in the distribution of our Indian population, to those who regard their presence as a detriment, Colorado seems to have been much more fortunate than many of her sister States.8

COLORADO'S CONTINUING EFFORTS TO EXCLUDE INDIAN HISTORY, CULTURE AND SOCIAL CONTRIBUTUIONS FROM ITS 22-2-104(2) CIVICS COURSE IS A CONTINUATION OF THESE 1800s ETHNIC CLEANSING POLICIES.

THE STATE, INCLUDING THE CDE, IS COMPLICIT IN DENYING AMERICAN INDIAN'S RIGHTS TO A 22-1-104(2) COURSE.

SHAME ON COLORADO.

Part 1: Notes

1. https://fordhaminstitute.org/sites/default/files/publication/pdfs/20210623-state-state-standards-civics-and-us-history-20210.pdf (accessed online September 5, 2021).
https://www.coloradopolitics.com/opinion/the-podium-colorado-schools-flunk-history/article_ebf7c332-fa6b-11eb-9424-07833425e760.html (accessed online September 5, 2021).

2. https://www.facebook.com/630KHOW/videos/amber-northern-joins-ross/12171366420669409/ June 24, 2021 (accessed online September 5, 2021).

3. Colorado Department of Education Cites to 22-1-104 or HB 19-1192
Social Studies, July 1, 2021
www.cde.state.co.us/cosocialstudies (accessed online July 10, 2021).
Graduation Guidelines, August 11, 2021
https://www.cde.state.co.us/postsecondary/graduationguidelines (accessed online August 20, 2021).
Graduation Guidelines Flexibility for the Class of 2021, August 11, 2021
https://www.cde.state.co.us/postsecondary/graduationguidelinesflexibilityaugust2020-2021pdf (accessed online August 20, 2021).
Graduation Guidelines Frequently Asked Questions for Class of 2021, August 4, 2021
https://www.cde.state.co.us/postsecondary/graduationguidelinesfrequentlyaskedquestionsforclassof2021 (accessed online August 20, 2021).
Graduation Guidelines (GG): Frequently Asked Questions
https://www.cde.state.co.us/postsecondary/detailedfaqggreporting (accessed online March 3, 2021).
Reporting Graduation Guidelines PWR Town Hall, February 23, 2021
https://drive.google.com/drive/folders/1KmKcA7wGG_VlTrCFlmxG5MDvSUWHzlsI (accessed online March 23, 2021).
CO DOE Graduation Guidelines Engagement Toolkit
§§ 22-1-104(2) Compliance Required – State Legislated Civics Course
https://www.cde.state.co.us/postsecondary/

graduationguidelinesengagementtoolkit (accessed online March 3, 2021).
Graduation Guidelines Flexibility for the Class of 2021
https://www.cde.state.co.us/postsecondary/graduationguidelinesflexibilityaugust2020-2021pdf (accessed online March 3, 2021).
Graduation Guidelines Flexibility for the Class of 2021
https://www.cde.state.co.us/postsecondary/graduationguidelinesflexibility2020-2021pdf (accessed online March 3, 2021).
Graduation Guidelines Frequently Asked Questions for Class of 2021
https://www.cde.state.co.us/postsecondary/
graduationguidlinesfrequentlyaskedquestionsforclassof2021 (accessed online March 3, 2021).
CO DOE Graduation Guidelines § § 22-1-104
Compliance Required COVID-19 and Graduation 2021
www.cde.state.co.us/postsecondary/graduationguidelines (accessed online March 3, 2021).
Guidelines § § 22-1-104
Compliance Required COVID-19
https://www.cde.state.co.us/postsecondary/graduationguidlinesfaqs (accessed online March 3, 2021).
Contact Person for Graduation Questions: https://www.cde.state.co.us/cdegen/keycontactsatcde (accessed online March 3, 2021).

4. CO DOE District Accountability Handbook, September 2020; https://www.cde.state.co.us/accountability/district-accountability-handbook-2020_final_9-10-2020 (accessed online July 10, 2021).

5. Colorado State Board of Education School District Accreditation Contract https://www.cde.state.co.us/uip/lisa-medlers-email-communications-with-sample-contract-june-2021 (accessed online July 10, 2021).

6. https://www.cpr.org/2021/09/30/colorado-students-arent-supposed-to-graduate-without-earning-about-indigenous-history-and-culture-are-they/ (accessed December 18, 2021).

7. Jaramillo, Nathalia E. Arizona, Hannibal's Cowboys, and the Modern Day Tie-Down, Pages 119-124, Published online: Dec. 11, 2012 (accessed May 18, 2021).

8. Report of the Commissioner of Indian Affairs to the Secretary of the Interior, United States. Office of Indian Affairs, U.S. Government Printing Office, 1891.

Colorado Springs Diversity Program Paused

Some School Systems Pause Diversity Programs Amid Pushback Posted on February 26, 2022 (Accessed online March 1, 2022)

Carolyn Thompson and Heather Hollingsworth, Associated Press, February 20, 2022

Conservative takeovers of local school boards have already altered lessons on race and social injustice in many classrooms. Now some districts are finding their broader efforts on diversity, equity and inclusion are also being challenged.

As her Colorado school district's equity director, Alexis Knox-Miller thought the work she and a volunteer team were doing was on solid ground, especially with an audit in hand that detailed where the district was falling short in making sure all students had the same opportunities.

But in December, Knox-Miller reluctantly disbanded the equity leadership team after more than a year of meetings. New conservative members had won a majority on the school board after voicing doubts about the work, and she worried the efforts might not lead anywhere.

The new board says it will take up the issue in the spring.

https://www.amren.com/news/2022/02/some-school-systems-pause-diversity-programs-amid-pushback/ (Accessed online March 1, 2022).

Colorado Sphinx Diversity Program Paused

Some School Sudden Pause Diversity Programs Amid Backlash, Boxed on February 20, 2022/At cased online March 5, 2022.

Carolyn Thompson and Heather Hollingworth, Associated Press, February 20, 2022

Conservative takeovers of local school boards have often ushered changes to race and social climate in recent classrooms. Now some districts are finding their broader efforts on diversity and inclusion may also being challenges.

At the Colorado school district's equity director, Alesha Knox Miller, thought the work she and a volunteer team were doing was on solid ground, opening with up to make inclusion a said aimed where she decides was falling short in making sure all students had the same opportunities.

But in December, Knox Miller reluctantly welcomed the routine reassigning to a role more than a year of it evolving. New conservative members who took up majority on the school board are not sure to what about the work, and she worried the efforts might now lead anywhere.

"The new board says it will take up the issue in the spring."

https://www.thegazette.com/news/2022-02-20-preschool-dismantle-program-diversity-program-amid-pushback-k-2/accessed online March 5, 2022.

190 /

www.ingramcontent.com/pod-product-compliance
Lightning Source LLC
Chambersburg PA
CBHW011955150426
43199CB00020B/2869